Shipwrecked Lives

BY

NICHOLAS KINSEY

Copyright © 2018 by Nicholas Kinsey
All rights reserved. This book or any portion thereof
may not be reproduced or used in any manner whatsoever
without the express written permission of the publisher
except for the use of brief quotations in a book review.

Printed on acid-free paper

Second Edition, October 2023
ISBN 978-1-7381687-1-2

Cinegrafica Films & Publishing
820 Rougemont
Quebec, QC G1X 2M5
Canada
Tel. 418-652-3345

In memory of my mother
Winifred Mary Pryce

FOREWORD

I am a Canadian and British writer and director of film and television drama. I started work on a film version of *Shipwrecked Lives* back in the 1980s and so it has been well over thirty years now that I have been drawn to this fascinating story. The *Empress of Ireland* passenger liner sank after a collision with a Norwegian collier in the St. Lawrence River on a foggy night in May 1914, claiming the lives of 1,012 people. The *Commission of Inquiry* into the disaster pitted a multinational transport industry giant against a tiny Norwegian coal-hauling firm and was, without a doubt, one of the most interesting maritime inquiries ever. Unfortunately, my plans for a film version never got off the ground, but I have enjoyed every moment of writing this novel.

The novel required extensive historical research and is largely based on the 2,000 pages of testimony at the Inquiry. This novel is based on a lot of well-known facts and, of course, when the facts are not available the writer's job is to invent. This book remains a work of historical fiction.

'The world is what it is, men who are nothing, who allow themselves to become nothing, have no place in it.'

       V.S. Naipaul

'I think that the sinking of the *Empress* was worse. On the *Titanic*, it was the waiting that was hard. There was no wait at all on the *Empress*. You just had time to think what you had to do and to do it. The *Titanic* went down like a baby going to sleep. The *Empress* rolled over like a pig in the mud.'

       William Clark

LEXICON OF NAUTICAL TERMS

aft:	the back of a ship
bow:	the front of a ship
masthead lights:	two white lights with the front masthead light lower than the stern masthead light
port:	left side of ship looking forward (showing a red light)
porting or hard to port (hard-a-port):	turning to starboard (to the right) by bringing the tiller to port with the rudder going to starboard
starboarding or hard to starboard:	turning to port (to the left) by bringing the tiller to starboard with the rudder going to port
starboard:	right side of ship looking forward (showing a green light)
stern:	the back part of a ship
whistle or horn:	signals a ship's movement
a prolonged blast:	means that a ship is making way under power in fog
three short blasts:	means that a ship is stopping its forward movement by running the engines astern
two long blasts:	means that a ship is not moving but lying still in the water

One

May 29, 1914

A long blast from the ship's whistle awakened Tiria Townshend in her berth. She turned over in bed and then got up to look out of the porthole at the dark night. A heavy fog was blowing in near the ship, and all that was visible was the edge of the lower promenade deck. A second long blast was heard from the ship's whistle.

Tiria was a young New Zealand woman travelling to England with her Aunt Wynnie in the berth just across from her. She returned to her bed just as three short blasts were heard on the ship's whistle. She gave up any thought of sleep and lay wide-awake listening to the sounds of the ship.

The passenger liner had started to slow down, going through the thick fog. On the bow of the proud vessel, one could read: *EMPRESS OF IRELAND*. She was the sister ship to the *Empress of Britain* and was a fast ship on the North Atlantic run.

A second series of three short blasts was heard. Tiria supposed that passenger liners blew their whistles all the time on the St. Lawrence River as a greeting of some kind, or perhaps it was customary in a fog. Still, it was very annoying and made sleep impossible. She glanced at her aunt and saw her stir fitfully in her berth. At that moment the ship's engine faltered briefly and then she heard a long blast coming, presumably from another ship.

"What was that?" Wynnie asked, rubbing her eyes.

"It's a fog horn, Auntie," Tiria said, "we're going through fog."

There was a sudden change in the engine noise as the ship started to move again.

On the bridge, Captain Kendall yelled through a megaphone at a collier which had suddenly appeared out of the fog, heading straight for the starboard side of the passenger liner.

"Go back, go back."

Moments later, the two ships collided in the fog. The *Storstad* bow cut into the side of the *Empress* like a knife going through butter. Steel sliced through steel to a depth of 18 feet. A bronze plaque from the *Empress* cabin number 328 fell noisily onto the bow of *Storstad*.

"Keep your engines full speed ahead," shouted Kendall in desperation at the *Storstad*. "Keep full speed ahead."

The *Storstad* officers ran out onto the bridge of their ship as Captain Anderson in the wheelhouse attempted to keep the nose of the collier in the side of the *Empress*, but it was a useless manoeuvre as the two ships quickly separated in the fog.

In her cabin, Tiria got up and went to the porthole, looking out briefly, but the ship remained enveloped in the fog.

"Something's happening, Auntie."

Tiria opened the cabin door to pandemonium. She saw several passengers milling about in the hallway and others emerging from their cabins. Some were going up to the promenade deck to take a look. An assistant steward was lighting the gas lamps and moving down the hall.

"Is everything all right?" asked an elderly woman.

"Of course, ma'am," the steward replied.

The woman returned to her cabin as the steward disappeared from view. Tiria stepped back inside to find her aunt sitting up in bed.

"What's going on, dear?"

"I don't know. I think we hit something."

There was a sudden listing to starboard and Tiria lost her balance before grabbing the side of her berth.

"Let's get dressed and go have a look," Tiria said.

She put on her coat, stockings and shoes as Wynnie got up and started to pull on her coat.

From the hall, they could hear a loud male voice going from door to door. A knock was heard at their door and the voice announced: "EVERYBODY OUT."

Tiria rushed to open the door and saw Chief Steward Gaade, pulling on his white jacket, as he went down the hall. The first-class passengers were standing around, holding canvas and cork lifebelts in their arms.

"Get your lifebelts on and go out on deck," Gaade yelled to the passengers. A panicked woman grabbed his arm.

"Have we struck an iceberg?" the woman asked.

"Please save us," another woman cried.

"No one will be saved unless you go out on the deck and get in the boats," Gaade insisted.

Tiria slammed the door and quickly finished dressing.

"Come on Auntie, we've got to get out of here. Hurry up."

SHIPWRECKED LIVES

Wynnie put on her shoes and stood up.

"I'm ready, dear."

Tiria grabbed her aunt by the arm and pulled her towards the door as the floor of the cabin tilted at an angle. The door swung open, slamming them both up against the wall. Together, they scrambled up the inclined floor and left the cabin.

The corridor was almost empty as Tiria and her aunt headed for the promenade deck, bouncing off the side wall due to the list of the ship. They struggled up the almost vertical stairs to the boat deck on the starboard side, where they could hear a lot of shouting and people milling about.

Tom Bingham held his little family close and desperately looked for a safe way off the ship. It was a miracle they had gotten this far. They had been travelling in second class, several decks below first class, and it had been just that much further for them to reach the boat deck.

Tom and Alice were young, strong, and driven by the need to get their little boy Jamie to safety. They had been wakened by the ship's whistles and struggled to dress the sleeping child before leaving their cabin. They had to fight their way through the crowded passageways and the stairwells made hazardous by the list of the ship.

Now Tom looked at the chaos on the boat deck and wondered if they were going to be saved at all. Several steel lifeboats on davits were being lowered into the water, but an impenetrable mob of desperate passengers was already clamouring for places on them. He dragged his wife and son over to a railing and then went in search of lifebelts. The list of the ship was worse by the time he got back.

"I could only find two," Tom said. "Put one on Jamie and another on yourself."

Alice put Jamie in the lifebelt and had to double it around him due to his small size. She had to brace herself by putting a foot on the railing to avoid falling overboard. Many passengers had already fallen off the slippery deck into the water.

Nearby, the crew was busy lowering a lifeboat full of frightened women and children into the water some thirty feet below. In the river, there were some twenty passengers who had escaped from a capsized lifeboat and were struggling to stay afloat among debris from the ship.

Alice finished attaching Jamie's lifebelt and then held the other one out to her husband.

"I can swim, Tom. You put it on."

"No, you put it on. Do it now," Tom insisted. "I'll hold Jamie."

He put his arms around the child and grabbed the railing. Alice had just finished putting on her lifebelt when she suddenly lost her balance and flipped over the railing into the water. There was nothing Tom could do but watch, horrified at the disappearance of his wife.

Tiria had pulled her aunt away from the chaos on the starboard side. It had been an uphill struggle against the list of the ship, but somehow they had managed to climb to the port side railing. On the way, they had run into an assistant steward who was busy distributing lifebelts. Tiria had been lucky to get the last one after having struggled with a man holding several in his arms.

People screamed as the ship listed dangerously in the water.

Tiria looked down the way they had come. It seemed like an almost vertical drop to the starboard side. The ship was sinking fast and was almost on its side. Tiria and Wynnie climbed over the port side railing and walked down the side of the ship over the portholes.

Wynnie stopped briefly to look at a small boy's panicked face looking out at them from a porthole. She thought about the frightened child and his parents, who had no chance of escaping the sinking ship. They had barely had time to escape themselves from their cabins in first class, but there was no hope for those with cheap accommodations in steerage. Tiria pulled her aunt away, and they continued down the side of the ship towards the water.

Most of the steel lifeboats on the port side were stuck on their davits and unmovable, while several Englehardt collapsible wooden lifeboats had been cut free and were drifting on the water. Knots of terrified passengers gathered near the waterline in their lifebelts hoping to get into one of the drifting wooden boats.

Tiria thrust the lifebelt on her aunt.

"Put this on, Auntie."

"I can't accept it, Tiria. You put it on."

"Auntie, please. We're going into the water. You can't swim. I can swim, in fact, I am an excellent swimmer. Give me your coat."

Tiria helped her aunt off with the coat and put on the lifebelt, attaching it at the front. She helped her aunt remove her shoes.

"I love you, dear," Wynnie said.

"I love you too," Tiria said. "We're going to be all right, you'll see."

Wynnie was frozen with fear as she stood at the edge of the

water, watching Tiria pull off her shoes.

"Tell Brian I love him. I'll miss him."

"I will, Auntie. I'll tell Uncle Brian, I'll tell everyone."

Suddenly, the ship lurched to starboard as the funnels struck the water with a loud crash and a cry went up from the passengers. Tiria and her aunt slipped off the ship into the water as a load of rigging and debris cascaded down the port side.

Two

The *Empress of Ireland* passenger liner had gone down fast, the suction from her massive hull dragging a large number of people down with her. She sank in only 14 minutes and there was little hope for survival among the passengers in second and third class.

In the dark, cries could be heard from passengers struggling to stay afloat on the black water of the St. Lawrence. A heavy steel lifeboat appeared out of the fog with a sailor on the bow holding a kerosene lantern, illuminating the water. The men were pulling survivors into the boat as fast as they could find them. Nearby in the thick fog, Tiria struggled with her coat as she looked around for her aunt, who had disappeared from view.

"Wynnie...Wynnie," Tiria called out as she swam in circles trying to locate her aunt. She swam near a man wearing a lifebelt and pushing a floating suitcase.

"Can you help me pull off my coat, please?" Tiria asked the man. He took pity on her and swam closer.

"Here, take the case," he said.

Tiria grabbed the case for support as the man pulled the wet coat off one shoulder. She dumped the coat as she climbed onto the case.

"Thank you, sir," Tiria said, but the man had already

disappeared behind a wave in the fog. The lantern of a Norwegian lifeboat appeared dimly out of the fog. Tiria abandoned the case and swam towards the boat.

In the dawn light, a farmer and his wife were driving along the coast road in a horse-drawn wagon to the market in St. Luce, when they stopped to look at the figure of a woman walking on the shore.

It was a very strange sight so early in the morning. The woman was wearing a torn shift and was naked from the waist up. She had very white skin and long auburn hair down her back as she walked east along the beach into the sunlight.

The husband and wife glanced at each other, unsure whether their eyes were deceiving them.

"*Qui est là?*" the woman asked her husband.

"*Je ne sais pas, ma chère,*" he said, "but it is quite unusual to see someone walking naked on the beach so early in the morning."

The farmer secured the reins and climbed down from the wagon.

"She needs our help, the poor woman," the wife said in a charitable tone.

"Maybe she's a crazy woman," the husband said with a naughty grin, "or perhaps a Protestant temptress put there by the devil."

The wife laughed at the dark humour of her husband.

"*Le père Simard* might say that, but I think she's a real person, not a ghost. Take the blanket."

The husband set off after the woman, who appeared to be in a daze as she stumbled along the beach in her bare feet, talking to herself.

SHIPWRECKED LIVES

"Mademoiselle, vous avez froid. Please, take the blanket."

Alice glanced at the man following her, covering her breasts with her arms and shivering from the cold. She lurched away from him. He watched her go and his heart went out to her. Something terrible had happened to this young woman. She was wet and cold and unstable on her legs, like a boxer who had just received a knockout punch and was struggling to maintain her equilibrium before collapsing.

The man stopped and looked back at his wife, raising his arms in a sign of frustration. After a moment of indecision, he decided to take matters into his own hands and ran after Alice. He seized her in the blanket after wrestling her to the ground.

"Vous parlez français?"

The woman shook her head.

"You speak English?"

Alice lost consciousness in the man's arms.

The wagon drove along a street in the town of Rimouski and pulled up at the portico of the Ursuline monastery on Notre Dame Street. The monastery was an impressive building perched on the heights, with a view overlooking the St. Lawrence River. The Ursuline sisters were the first Catholic nuns to land in the New World. They ran schools and cared for the sick and the needy across the continent.

The farmer and his wife climbed down and helped Alice in her blanket into the foyer. Once inside the dark entrance, they were met by a sister in a black habit who whispered something to them in French. They sat down with the sister in an alcove and quickly explained the situation. The sister took pity on the poor English woman with the damp hair and blanket. She put her arm around Alice and thanked the farmer and his wife. She led Alice away to the infirmary as the couple left the building.

In the infirmary, the sister sat Alice down in a corner and went looking for clean clothes. She returned with the clothes and an older sister, who put a cup of hot tea in front of Alice and helped her to dress. The clothes were worn and had holes in them, but they were warm and comfortable.

Alice, in a white blouse and grey wool cardigan, drank her tea as the two sisters tried to make conversation.

"*Madame, vous êtes une rescapée du bateau?*"

Alice nodded.

"*Comment êtes vous arrivée sur la plage?*"

"*La plage*, you mean the beach?"

The sisters nodded enthusiastically before Alice shook her head, unable to reply to the question.

A third sister arrived with a bowl of soup and a crust of bread. Alice was ravenous and quickly ate the food under the sisters' watchful eyes. After she had finished the soup and eaten a portion of the bread, she suddenly stood up, looking very agitated, and ran out of the infirmary.

The sisters watched her go as their mother superior, an older woman wearing spectacles, stepped into the room from the stairwell.

"*Où est-elle?*"

The sisters pointed to the chapel down the hall.

"*Elle est partie en courant, mère*. She ran away."

The mother superior followed Alice and found her looking very agitated in the chapel. In the dark interior, Alice was marching up and down and talking to herself.

"Jamie, come to mummy," Alice demanded of the voice in her head. "I told you to come back!"

The mother superior stepped into the chapel and gently took Alice by the arm.

"Miss, I speak English," she said. "How are you feeling?"

Alice said nothing as the woman led her back to the infirmary. The sisters sat Alice down again as the mother superior questioned her.

"You were on the ship?"

"The ship?"

"Yes, the passenger liner, dear. Everyone in town is talking about the sinking of the ship."

Alice looked down at a button on her cardigan hanging by a thread and started to pull on it. She appeared to not understand the question.

Three

After dark, Alice was taken in an open buggy to the railway station by the monastery driver. She had on an old woollen coat and seemed alert as she sat next to the driver. The horse trotted up to the station door and stopped. The driver came around to help her climb down and then led her into the building.

"*Attention à la marche, madame.*"

They climbed the stairs and entered a crowded waiting room. They wound their way across the floor, filled with groups of men talking in loud voices and foreign tongues, and descended the stairs to a large room in the basement, which had been turned into a makeshift dormitory for the surviving women and children from the ship. The women sat on foldable beds talking in whispers, as the children played together nearby. Intermittent sobbing could be heard, coming from the dark recesses of the room. A woman with an apron appeared carrying a tray full of cups of tea.

"*Merci, Georges.* I'll look after her now."

"*Bonsoir, madame,*" said the driver as he left.

The *Empress of Ireland* had belonged to the Canadian Pacific

SHIPWRECKED LIVES

Railway (CPR) along with her sister ship the *Empress of Britain*. The ships were built on the Clyde in Scotland with Liverpool as their home port. The *Empress* brand of passenger liners travelled the oceans of the world, linking Liverpool to Quebec City and New York, Vancouver to Hong Kong, Yokohama, Sydney and Auckland. *Empress* ships offered the ultimate experience in trans-Atlantic or trans-Pacific travel. It was almost inconceivable that such a prestigious passenger liner could be lost at sea.

The news of the disaster had travelled like wildfire. During the first twelve hours, a lot of misinformation circulated in the press. When the news arrived in Liverpool on the afternoon of May 29, they were reporting that every passenger had been saved. CPR offices around the world were besieged by people who wanted to know whether a relative or crew member had been saved. As the actual numbers of lost lives started to come out, there was enormous public pressure to get the story right.

The town of Rimouski situated at the mouth of the Rimouski River in the Gaspé peninsula was soon besieged by journalists from around the world. They arrived by train on the Grand Trunk (GTR) rail line from Montreal in the west and from Moncton and Halifax in the east. They gathered at the pier, east of the town opposite St. Barnaby Island, waiting for the boats bringing in the bodies of the dead on the high tide.

A steamer arrived and started to unload the cadavers from the wreck, laying them out in pyramid shapes on the dock with the adults on the bottom and the children on top. The faces of the victims were swollen and bruised from floating in the river. There was a great state of agitation among the survivors and their families as they pressed forward, looking for their loved ones. The journalists were quickly pushed aside by the curious townspeople who had never witnessed such horrors before in their small community.

Alice advanced mechanically down the long rows of bodies peering furtively at the contorted faces of the dead. At the end of the pier, she suddenly burst into tears.

"I can't find them," Alice sobbed.

A sailor by the name of James Galt approached Alice.

"There's still the *Lady Evelyn* out there, missus. It'll be back in no time."

"They're both missing, my husband and my son."

"Well, I'm sure they're doin' their best to find them. Come back to the station. We'll get you a hot cuppa tea."

Galt took her arm and led her away from the crowd along the road to the railway station. Near a coal shed, several local children in rags were playing hopscotch. One girl stood out from the rest. Blonde and full of life, five-year-old Vicky Hayes wore a woman's cardigan that practically touched the ground. She had survived the disaster and was waiting for her parents to arrive.

Captain Kendall of the *Empress* was a survivor. Unshaven and leaning on a cane for support, he had insisted on filing past the rows of bodies on the dock. He was trailed by Johnson, his exasperated first officer.

"I'm the captain, Edward," Kendall said, "I have the right to see every bloody corpse I want to."

"You're making a fool of yourself. There's no point to it, Henry."

"I have to, I have to see them."

Kendall pulled away from Johnson and moved down the dock towards a woman, weeping over her dead husband. The woman looked up as Kendall approached.

"You the captain of the ship?" the grieving woman asked him and he nodded wearily.

"Well, you should be downright ashamed of yerself. You kilt me husband, damn you, man."

The woman spat at the captain, who stepped back in shock. To his relief, Johnson arrived and led him away.

"What's the good of being a whipping post for these poor folk?" Johnson said. "It won't bring back their loved ones, that's for sure. Leave 'em in peace, I say."

Kendall was speechless as they left the crowd on the dock.

"I had a talk with Murphy, sir," Johnson said, "he'll go along with whatever you have to say. The other men will back you anytime."

"I sent my report to Walters. He…" Kendall stopped in mid-sentence and looked off into space.

"You did your best, sir," Johnson said.

The two men looked at each other in silence. Kendall felt ashamed and humiliated by the bodies on the pier while his colleague seemed quite unaffected by the ordeal.

Alice Bingham lay on a cot in the makeshift dormitory at the station and tried to have a nap. Finally, she gave up and struggled to her feet. She made her way among the sleeping bodies towards the exit where she noticed a little blonde girl playing with a doll.

"Shouldn't you be resting?" Alice asked.

"I don't want to miss my mummy," Vicky mumbled, sitting cross-legged on a cot. "Dolly wants to go for a walk."

"She's very pretty. My name's Alice, what's your name?"

"Vicky."

"How old are you, Vicky?"

"Five."

"I'm going upstairs, do you want to come with me?"

Vicky got up, collected her doll and gave Alice her hand. Together they climbed the stairs to the waiting room where the men were lodged and then walked through the crowd on the platform to the canteen.

In the canteen Alice ordered a hot chocolate for Vicky and herself. They sat down in silence at a table, observing each other over the steam from their cups. Vicky took a spoon from the saucer and fiddled with it, playing at feeding her doll spoonfuls of hot chocolate.

"My mum and dad are coming to fetch me tomorrow."

"They are, are they?"

"My mum has red hair, your hair is brown."

"My hair is auburn, reddish-brown. You can see the red tint in it, if you look carefully."

Vicky held a blonde curl in her hand, smiling.

"My hair is blonde."

"Yes, it is, and it's lovely."

Vicky drank her chocolate, observing her new friend.

Captain Kendall and First Officer Johnson were lodged in an old farmhouse near the edge of town belonging to the local CPR agent. The plan was to keep the captain and the first officer of the *Empress* away from any journalists who might be looking for a story in the small town.

"Walters is worried about the inquest tomorrow," Johnson said, sitting at the kitchen table drinking tea in the fading light. "He thinks that it is a sight too early. People are demanding it, so the newspapers are sending their reporters here."

"Did you see the face of that woman on the dock?" Kendall

asked, looking exhausted.

"Don't you worry about her, sir. She's just an old bag, lost her man, that's all. Forget it."

Kendall sighed and said nothing as the yellow light from an oil lamp flickered across his tired face.

"Would you like a drink?" Johnson asked. "Got a good scotch whisky from the harbour master. It'll do you a world of good, old chap, keep yer mind together."

Johnson stood up to get two glasses and poured the whisky. He handed a glass to Kendall, who pushed it away.

"Drink it later if you like, sir. Nothing like good, hard liquor. Mustn't waste it, that's what I say."

Kendall closed his eyes as Johnson drank his whisky.

"When a ship goes down, that's the hand of fate," Johnson murmured. "Fate's a sly bastard, he is, always doing what's least expected. I say it's no fault of the skipper or the crew when a ship goes down."

Johnson looked over at Kendall, who had fallen asleep in his chair from exhaustion.

Four

Coroner Pinault and his fellow jurors, mainly local officials and tradesmen, listened intently to a dishevelled Captain Kendall, who stood up to testify in the tiny Rimouski schoolhouse. The grey-haired jurors sat at a long table with Pinault and a translator at the centre, facing the crowd sitting on benches. Behind the captain sat the CPR superintendent Walters, looking very uneasy, as reporters scribbled notes and survivors exchanged glances.

"When we were hit amidships," Kendall said, slurring his words, "I shouted from the bridge 'keep full speed ahead' through a megaphone."

Nearby, an interpreter translated simultaneously for the francophone jury.

"*Il a crié dans un porte-voix 'garder pleine vitesse avant'.*"

"If he had kept his nose in the hole, we could've beached her," Kendall said.

The interpreter translated the captain's words as the coroner prepared to ask a question.

"*Capitaine*, when the *Storstad* came out of the hole, what happened?"

"She slipped away on our starboard side and disappeared in the fog," Kendall said. "We started to list almost immediately."

"Maybe *Capitaine* Andersen did not hear your call?"

"Even if the man did not hear my call, sir, he had to do it," Kendall said, his face flushed with anger. "Any sailor knows that."

He coughed violently as Coroner Pinault looked at his notes and consulted a juror.

"I've some questions here about the rescue of the passengers," he remarked. "Dr Grant has testified that he saw the *Storstad* boats full to capacity with survivors. He says they did their best."

"Their best?" Kendall shouted, red-faced with anger. "No, sir! They abandoned us in the fog. Their boats arrived too late to do anything. We had no assistance. We saved as many as we could while they stood by."

The interpreter stumbled over his words as he tried to keep pace with Kendall's angry outburst. The jurors waited impatiently for the translation while most of the audience, who understood English, were shocked by Kendall's comments.

"But *Capitaine*, I have heard several reports saying the contrary, that the Norwegians provided assistance," Pinault insisted.

A wave of protests was heard in the crowd.

"The Norwegians did nothing!" a bearded man yelled.

"It's their fault," a fat man bellowed from the back.

"The Norwegians are to blame," another man cried.

Their shouts set off a wave of loud protests and angry gestures from every corner of the room.

Pinault banged his gavel in an ineffectual attempt to maintain order, but was ignored in the rising chaos. Several reporters dashed out of the room to file their stories.

In the audience, Walters observed Kendall's angry profile nervously. Clearly, the captain was a disturbed man and his irrational behaviour in the schoolroom did not augur well for the impending inquiry in Quebec City. Walters couldn't imagine Kendall defending the interests of the CPR in any official capacity.

Godefroy Paradis was a fisherman and *caboteur* from *Anse-aux-Coques* near Rimouski. He had been hired by the CPR office at *Pointe-au-Père* in the early morning hours of the disaster to search for bodies on the river. The *Rose des Vents* had arrived in the debris field, along with the steamer, the *Lady Evelyn,* and the pilot boat, the *Eureka*. It had been hard work hauling the floating corpses into the boat. As the morning progressed, the steamers had disappeared from view and only a handful of fishing boats remained on the horizon.

After several long days and nights on the river, Godefroy was tired and stiff as he sat at the tiller of the schooner. Unshaven and sporting a large moustache, Godefroy was looking his age. He had just returned from several days of fishing when he was hired by the company, along with his two sons, Thomas and Louis.

It had rained in the morning, but now the wind had dropped and the river was like glass under sunny skies. Thomas stood on the bow, scanning the huge debris field for floaters.

"*Encore une passe,* then we go north," Godefroy said.

Louis appeared from below decks with a cup of tea, which he handed to his father. Thomas pointed to some debris on their starboard side.

"*Regarde à tribord, Père.*"

Godefroy stood up and looked through his binoculars. He brought the schooner around and they headed off towards the floating debris. They approached a corpse floating on the water. Louis snagged the body with the gaff while his brother attempted to pull it closer to the boat.

"*Prends le sous les bras!*" Godefroy shouted from his place at the tiller.

Thomas had already hooked his feet on the railing and was leaning out over the water, his body half out of the boat.

"I'll lift him," Thomas said, reaching under the man's arms. "You grab the legs."

Louis dropped the gaff on the deck and together they hauled the swollen corpse aboard. The deck was already loaded with more than a dozen bodies in various states of decomposition.

"Good work, boys. Now let's get that sail up."

Thomas started to raise the mainsail as Godefroy brought the bow of the schooner into the wind. They were soon beating a course to windward, heading west back into the debris field.

Five

The Empress was listing to starboard at a dangerous angle. Passengers were standing on the railing and holding on as best they could. Kendall was on the bridge, looking down as his men attempted to load the lifeboats. Below him, he noticed a man with a little boy in a sailor suit perched over the water and hanging on for dear life. Suddenly the ship's rigging collapsed and tumbled down onto their heads, knocking the man into the river, but somehow leaving the child alone clinging to the railing. He looked down and saw the boy imploring his father to come back, but couldn't move to help him.

Kendall woke up from the nightmare, sitting in a battered armchair in the dark. He held his throbbing head in his hands. There was a half-empty bottle of whisky on the dresser near an oil lamp. He got up and limped awkwardly across the room to get a drink.

In the mirror, he caught the reflection of an unshaven wreck of a man and backed away in a panic. He put on his captain's jacket and stepped in front of the mirror. There he was again, that imposter of a captain, a hopeless failure in life who had caused the death of thousands of innocents. In a frenzy, he ripped off the gold epaulettes and angrily smashed the mirror with his fist.

SHIPWRECKED LIVES

It was mid-morning when a grey-haired insurance investigator knocked on the door of the farmhouse. The house was silent, so he knocked again and pushed the front door open. He stepped into the kitchen and noticed a tea service on the table. He was a small man with a furtive look, sporting a moustache and mutton chop sideburns.

"Hello, is anyone home?"

The investigator stepped into the main room and saw a man fully dressed, asleep on the bed in the corner. The floor was littered with shards of broken glass.

"Captain Kendall, is that you?"

Kendall coughed and turned over.

"Captain Kendall, are you all right, sir?"

Kendal groaned.

"It's been quite difficult locating you, sir. I'm Kenneth Ashby. I work for a group of insurance companies in New York."

"What the hell are you doing here?" Kendall grumbled as he sat up with hair tousled.

"I came on the train yesterday. I'm here to investigate several insurance claims regarding the shipwreck."

"So this is a private affair?"

"Yes, indeed. I'm sorry for the loss of your ship, sir."

"Pour me some tea, would you, Mr Ashby?"

Ashby hesitantly returned to the kitchen and collected the tea tray put there earlier by the farmer's daughter. He poured the tea while Kendall got up and staggered over to the table.

"We were six on the bridge," Kendall said, taking the cup of tea from Ashby. "Only Quartermaster Murphy, First Officer Johnson and myself survived."

"It is quite rare to see so much loss of life in a collision and sinking, sir. This is quite unprecedented. The insurance companies are concerned that we have recovered so few bodies. Can you explain why this is the case?"

Kendall drank his tea and frowned.

"The ship went down in 14 minutes, Mr Ashby. If the *Storstad* had stayed in the hole..."

"Yes, I heard."

"We had no time. My officers and men were on the upper decks, helping passengers into lifeboats. They gave no thought to their personal safety."

"I see."

"I am not sure you do, sir. The ship listed to starboard moments after the collision. We couldn't get our boats out on the port side."

Ashby poured himself a cup of tea.

"The boat deck was swarming with passengers," Kendall said. "We had to drop many lifeboats in the water and fill them once they were free of the ship. We saved as many as we could."

"How did you save yourself?" Ashby asked.

"The funnels struck the water, and I fell overboard. When I came to the surface, I could see the line of the ship, the suction caused by the ship foundering and the two waves meeting in the middle. A man from a lifeboat called to me in the fog."

"Well, thank you, captain. I will tell my people in New York," Ashby said. "I would like to make a comment about the behaviour of your employees here in Rimouski. They are using the passenger lists to identify the survivors. I saw a journalist consulting the list yesterday. This will not do, sir."

Kendall was perplexed and didn't understand what Ashby was getting at. Ashby paused, exasperated.

"With a disaster of this size, captain," he continued, "and

the huge loss of life, you're going to have shysters and wagon-chasers claiming insurance policies on next of kin who were never anywhere near the ship. You understand? You must keep the passenger lists secret, sir."

"Better take it up with Mr Walters."

"He won't listen to me, sir. The number of claims will double when you get to Quebec."

"I don't think I can help you, sir. It is out of my hands. Walters is the man."

"Perhaps you can put in a word with him for me, captain. If we can keep the passenger list secret, we can weed out the fakers."

Six

The CPR had set up several tables in the Rimouski train station near the ticket office to provide assistance to the survivors of the shipwreck. There were numerous boxes of old clothes and blankets piled on the tables. There had been an outpouring of support from the local population and the clergy.

Alice approached an Ursuline sister in a long black habit, rummaging through a box of clothes for a mother and her child.

"Hello, sister. Have you seen a little blonde girl? Her name is Vicky."

The sister looked up at Alice.

"I'm not sure."

"I met her yesterday. She said she was waiting for her mother and father."

"I'm afraid I can't help you, miss."

"If you see her come in, my name is Alice Bingham. Tell her I will be down at the dock."

The sister smiled pleasantly and returned to her search.

"I'll keep an eye open for her, miss."

Several fishing boats were grouped together on the river

estuary some five miles offshore as a young Catholic priest said a mass for the dead to a crowd of local citizens and *Empress* crew members. The tanned and weathered faces of the fishermen and sailors clashed with the pale, hairless face of the priest. Several Empress crew members were present, along with James Galt, in the company of a pretty teenage girl named Françoise from *Pointe-au-Père*.

"*Je prie au père miséricordieux de faire venir une tempête pour libérer les corps, pour permettre aux familles d'enterrer leurs morts, in saecula saeculorum, amen.*"

As the priest finished his sermon, the teary-eyed crowd threw flowers on the water. The flowers floated among the air bubbles escaping from the wreck. A gasp was heard among the grieving crowd as they interpreted the air bubbles, breaking at the surface as a reply to the priest's sermon. The *Empress* lay some 130 feet below the surface on her starboard side, with strong currents playing a game of tug of war with her hull.

The ceremony was over and the fishing boats began to separate as they prepared to return to port with their load of sad passengers.

A train pulled into the Rimouski train station with its locomotive emitting noisy bursts of steam. The conductor walked up and down the platform, looking at his watch as passengers started to emerge from inside the station.

In the hall, there was a long lineup of people in front of a table where Walters and a CPR clerk by the name of Peters were checking the names of the passengers against the company list. Many of the survivors had bandages on their limbs as they stumbled forward in borrowed clothing and blankets.

"Keep it moving, please," Walters said, looking at his watch as a man stepped forward.

"Name, class and cabin number?" Peters murmured.

"William Barrie, second class. I can't remember the cabin number."

"Here he is," Peters said, checking the name off the list. "Go on, sir."

Standing nearby, the insurance investigator Ashby watched Barrie move off through the doors to the train as another passenger stepped forward.

James Galt entered the station and spotted Alice waiting in line next to a little girl clutching a doll.

"Mrs Bingham."

"Mr Galt, thank you so much for your support the other day. You were a great help."

"Ma'am, it was a pleasure. Are you planning on staying on in Quebec?"

"Yes, certainly."

"You mustn't lose hope. They're still searching. Who is this little one?"

Young Vicky piped up.

"Sir, I am not a little one. I am five years old."

"Well, well. You are quite the young lady then."

Alice raised her eyebrows and laughed.

Seven

"Gentlemen, I think you can see for yourselves the kind of slanderous things that are being written about my clients," John Griffin declared, holding up a newspaper. "We will not stand idly by while lies like this are being told. We are convinced that the *Empress of Ireland* is entirely responsible for the disaster."

It had not taken long for the A.F. Klaveness Line, owners of the *Storstad*, to respond to the sensational press reports following Captain Kendall's testimony at the inquest in Rimouski. On the advice of their New York solicitors, they had ordered their shipping agent to convene a press conference in a Montreal public room. Next to John Griffin sat Captain Thomas Andersen, a rough-looking man with a moustache, and his attractive blonde wife Frida.

A reporter stood up to ask a question.

"Mr Griffin, sir. Can you comment on Captain Kendall's statement to the press that your crew did not help save any lives?"

Griffin unfolded a newspaper so he could find the appropriate passage.

"Captain Kendall has said, and I quote: 'We had no assistance. We saved as many as we could while the Norwegians stood by. They abandoned us in the fog. Their boats arrived too late to do anything.'"

"Gentlemen," he said, "nothing could be further from the truth."

Griffin let the newspaper fall to the table in front of him as he glanced at Captain Andersen, who turned to address the crowd from his seat at the table.

"I am very unhappy," he said in a gruff voice, "this man tells a big lie. My men work very hard to save the passengers of the *Empress*."

He leaned toward his wife, who whispered in his ear.

"Yes, we give them our clothes, we feed them and we are treated this way. You will see. We will have an investigation and the truth will come out. Kendall is the guilty man."

Near the village of *Anse-aux-Coques*, Godefroy and the boys had come home for the evening meal and a wash up before heading out again. They had gone without sleep for several days and looked exhausted as they stumbled down from the wagon. Thomas unhitched the horse and led it into the barn as Godefroy and Louis headed towards the old stone farmhouse with its Norman-style gable roof and dormer windows.

As they entered the kitchen, the boys greeted their mother Justine, who stood at the stove ladling out the soup. Godefroy and the boys took their place at the table while the older girls, Françoise and Marie, served the men before serving the four children gathered around the table.

"I saw a lot of the survivors at the station, *Maman*," Françoise said. "Many of them are dressed in rags. They don't have any clothes."

"The women are in nightdresses and the children in pyjamas," Marie added.

"*Pauvres gens, Dieu nous protège,*" Justine said. "The *curé* has been around collecting clothing."

Godefroy and the boys listened quietly.

"The papers are talking about a thousand victims," Thomas said.

"*Le père Asselin* gave a mass on the river," Françoise said, "I went with them."

Justine looked up from the kitchen and exchanged a glance with Godefroy.

"*Maman,*" Marie said quickly, "I told her not to go, but she went anyway."

"You are such a spoilsport, Marie," Françoise said, infuriated by her sister.

Justine put more bread on the table as six-year-old Michel caught his dad's eye.

"*Père,* did you find any bodies?" Michel asked his dad.

"Yes, we did," Thomas said.

"Were they dead?"

"Course, they were, they were drowned," Louis said.

The children looked in silent awe at their older brothers.

Eight

Alice and Vicky had arrived at the Intercolonial GTR station in Levis on the south shore where the CPR had an office. A clerk at the counter was busy, handing out vouchers for free lodging and food for the passengers of the lost liner.

"Name, please," the clerk said.

A passenger murmured a name in a hushed voice to the clerk, who checked his name off the list and gave him a voucher. The queue moved slowly forward.

In a corner of the station, two Salvation Army women were serving soup to a group of listless survivors as a young man with a basket of apples approached the passengers in the queue and distributed the apples to outstretched hands.

Alice and Vicky soon collected their vouchers and exited the station. They crossed the road to the waterfront, where ferry boats were lined up to whisk passengers across the river to the Port of Quebec. A small wooden steamer with seats all around the lower deck had just tied up to the dock, and a man beckoned to them to come forward. They gave their tickets to the man and descended the gangway to the boat deck. Moments later, the little steamer took off across the river with a full load of passengers, many of them from the train station.

As they approached the city of Quebec from the river, they could see the magnificent *Château Frontenac* hotel above the

SHIPWRECKED LIVES

Dufferin Terrace and the Citadel fortifications on the hill. They entered the *Bassin Louise* in the lower town and were amazed by the number of watercraft in the harbour. There were schooners and *goélettes* coming and going under sail, large coastal steamers belching black smoke from their smokestacks, and small harbour runabouts carrying people here and there. Young Vicky was particularly taken by the little runabouts and waved at some girls her age who crossed their path.

Off to the right, in the deep-water harbour, there was a huge transatlantic liner loading passengers and cargo. The smell of coal and wood fires was omnipresent, and Alice held a scarf to her nose as they wound their way through the river traffic to the wharf.

Quebec City was a bustling metropolis in 1914 and a major port with a population of around 80,000 people. It was almost twice the size of Halifax and the gateway to Canada for a lot of newly arrived immigrants.

On a leafy street near the old town, Alice and Vicky climbed the stairs to an old Victorian house and knocked on the door. An elegant older woman with grey hair opened the door.

"*Entrez, s'il vous plaît*, I've been expecting you. I'm Pauline Pelletier. And you are?"

"Alice Bingham, madam, and this is Vicky, Vicky Hayes. We met in Rimouski."

Pauline was smoking a cigarette in a silver cigarette holder as she smiled at the pair in their threadbare clothes. She took the CPR chit from Alice and welcomed them into her home.

"Thank you, Miss Bingham. The child is..."

"The child is with me, Mrs Pelletier. The company has asked me to look after her until her parents or family take charge."

"I see," said Pauline, turning towards Vicky. "Well, we'll have to find you some clothes. We can't have you walking around like scarecrows."

Vicky looked amused.

"Scarecrows?"

"In French, we call them *"épouvantails"*, my dear. We use them to scare away the crows."

"Scare away the crows?" Vicky said with a grin. "But I'm not a scarecrow."

"No, you're not," Pauline said. "You are a little girl with lovely blonde locks. How old are you, pray tell?"

"Five," Vicky announced with a big smile.

"Five years old! Well, I never," exclaimed Pauline.

The women broke into a laugh.

"I go home!" Frida said angrily, standing in the doorway to the captain's cabin on the *Storstad*.

The argument had come out of thin air, a negative comment, an innocent remark, that meant next to nothing, and now Captain Andersen was trying desperately to reason with his wife. Frida was an intense, charismatic woman with a volatile nature. She was perspiring, with biceps bulging as she held the mop like a Roman mace ready for combat.

"It won't be long, my dear. We have a break until this is over. A couple of weeks, that's all."

Frida ignored her husband and returned to mopping the cabin floor.

"We'll be all right. You'll see," Andersen said, trying to reassure her.

"I go home!" Frida said. "I cannot take this life anymore. I scrub floors here or I scrub floors at home. It's the same."

"Back home, I have no job, Frida. You know that. You want me to be penniless? Is that what you want?"

"Get out!" Frida exploded, hurling the mop at her husband.

Andersen ducked, and the mop slammed into the wall behind him.

"You shouldn't do that, Frida. I'm your husband."

Captain Andersen looked up and saw a bemused John Griffin standing nearby watching the domestic drama unfold.

"Mr Griffin," he stammered with embarrassment, "please come with me. We go upstairs."

Frida picked up her mop and went back to work.

Nine

Pauline entered the upscale department store on *Côte de la Fabrique,* followed by Alice and a wide-eyed Vicky. A young salesman in a spiffy frock coat and waistcoat approached.

"We have come to see what you have on offer for the survivors of the *Empress*," Pauline said with a dignified air.

"Over here," the salesman said, going towards the back of the shop. He led the women to a pile of odd bits of clothing set out in several bins and on racks near the changing rooms. Alice checked the ragged clothing in the bin while Pauline looked at the poor quality coats on the racks.

"We're going to need a bit of everything: coats, dresses, underwear. Where are you hiding your best things, young man?"

"Madam, everything you see in the bin is free. It's for the survivors."

"But these are rags, cheap imitations made from very inferior material. Where are you keeping your good stuff?"

"This is all we have, madam," the salesman protested.

"I think we might want to have a chat with the manager. You must have more than this."

The salesman looked around nervously and then whispered in Pauline's ear.

"Well, I do have a few things around the corner."
"Ah...ha."
"If you'd care to take a look, madam."
Alice and Vicky looked amused as Pauline frowned at the man and then followed him into the storeroom.

James Galt was standing at the front desk in the decrepit lobby of the Neptune Hotel. He wet the end of a pencil as he wrote a letter to his mother on a piece of notepaper. A young bellhop with a nascent moustache appeared from a back room.
"Mr Galt. You're back."
"Yes, Pierre, I am."
"A man from the CPR office called. They want to see you as soon as possible."
Galt nodded and then stepped closer to look at the thin growth on the young man's upper lip.
"I see you've been growing your moustache, Pierre."
"Yes, I got the beeswax you recommended, but first I need to grow it out more."
"Well, it's coming along nicely. Got an envelope, have you, Pierre?"
The bellhop slipped a paper envelope onto the counter.
"Here you go. I hear that Williams didn't make it."
"You heard right," Galt said with a sad look on his face. "A very nice chap he was. We'll miss him."
He nodded at Pierre and took his leave.

Galt entered the CPR office, looking for superintendent Walters. A man wearing a waistcoat and a wide-brimmed visor was sitting at a desk, going over a ledger of accounts in front of the open door to a large, ornate office.

"I've come to see Mr Walters."

"What's it about?" Peters asked.

"Someone left a message for me to report in."

"Name, please."

"Galt, James."

Walters appeared in the doorway.

"Send him in, Peters. I'll see him."

Walters held the door open as Galt stepped inside and sat down.

"Mr Galt, I hear you were on deck at the time of the collision."

"Yes, sir. I was on the forward deck, having a smoke, when the *Storstad* ran into our ship. I want to make a statement."

"Yes, yes. Of course, you do. Why don't you tell me what you saw?"

"Well, sir, I already gave a statement to Mr Holden in Rimouski. You know Mr Holden?"

"Holden, of course, I do. He's been taking statements from the crew."

"Yes, sir. I would like to add something to my statement if I could."

"Look, Mr Galt, I think you've said quite enough. I've got some good news for you. We've arranged your passage on the *Montreal*. It's leaving this afternoon for Liverpool. Lucky man, you'll be home in a week."

Galt looked at Walters with frustration.

Ten

"Mummy will be happy to see my new dress," Vicky said. "Do you like it, Alice?"

"Yes, I do. You look lovely in it, dear."

Vicky and Alice were in the small bedroom on the second floor of Mrs Pelletier's house. Tucking in the child, Alice realized that the time would soon come when she would have to tell Vicky the truth.

"You smell like my mummy."

Alice smiled and then kissed the child.

"Sleep tight, dear."

Alice left the bedroom and went downstairs. The sitting room was in near darkness, illuminated by a single table lamp in the corner. Pauline was sitting in a leather club chair reading a book in French.

"How is she?"

"She's talking about seeing her mother."

Pauline got up and poured two small glasses of French brandy.

"I shouldn't be drinking," Alice said, "we are teetotallers you know. Tom wouldn't approve, but I cannot take it anymore."

She tilted the glass to her lips and drank it all at once, but it was too much for her. She choked and then recovered, coughing violently.

"*Santé*, cheers," Pauline said, smiling at Alice. "The brandy will do you good. I'm sure your husband would approve."

Pauline topped up Alice's glass. This time she took a smaller sip, letting the brandy tickle her throat.

"Tom was Salvation Army from way back," Alice said. "He played the clarinet in the band. There were some 170 of us on board the ship, all from Toronto. The band played in the dining room the night of the disaster. It was such a festive occasion. We were on our way to play at Prince Albert Hall in London."

"That's quite an honour, I'm sure."

"Yes, it is. I mean it was," Alice said, remembering the night on the ship.

The Salvation Army brass band played a familiar melody in the first-class dining room of the Empress. Alice and a group of army wives stood along the wall near the entrance watching the men play for the well-to-do passengers. Tom winked at Alice and seemed to be enjoying himself as the passengers dined on bone china and silver plate at the captain's table.

Captain Kendall came through the door and joined the guests at his table as the band played.

"I hope you enjoy the food. We have an excellent chef," Kendall said to his guests.

A distinguished-looking woman with pearls and a dark dress leaned towards the captain.

"Will we see any icebergs on this voyage, captain?"

"I doubt it. We sail too far south for that."

A handsome young man, smartly dressed with blond hair, playfully broke into the conversation.

"So you are not too worried about running into a mountain of ice, captain?"

"No. If you're thinking of the Titanic, we are much better equipped with lifeboats and our crew is trained for emergencies. There's no comparison."

"Captain, isn't it true that icebergs are often hardly visible at the surface?" asked an older man in a military uniform.

"Stop it, George. You terrible man," his wife scolded, "you'll make us all so very nervous."

A titter of laughter was heard from the adjoining tables. Kendall ignored the question and tasted the soup. It had been a very long day, and he suddenly felt very tired. His hand shook for no apparent reason, and he felt a headache coming on. He was looking forward to some time off and seeing his wife and child in England.

The Salvation Army band came to the end of their performance and the diners applauded as they marched out, followed by Alice and the army wives.

Alice looked up, embarrassed. She had drifted away down memory lane and wasn't sure how long she had been silent. Pauline sat quietly nearby, puffing away on her silver cigarette holder.

"Vicky still thinks her parents are coming to collect her," Alice said.

"Wait a day or two. Perhaps she needs to believe it, at least for a time," Pauline said.

"Do you really think so?"

"I do. Give her time. She's just a child. She may still be in a state of shock after what she's been through."

Eleven

The immigration hall on Pier 27 had, for most of the last century, been the port of entry into Canada for the legions of immigrants heading for a better life in Canada. Over half a million immigrants entered Canada through the Port of Quebec from 1869 to 1889. The hall on the Louise Embankment wharf with its wide verandah was over 400 feet long and could accommodate some 3,000 people at a time with its dining room, sleeping quarters and bathrooms. Inside the building were the offices of immigration, the port physician, medical services, customs, ticket sales, telegraph and telephone services. The immigrant had only to claim his or her baggage and embark on the special immigrant trains with their sleeping cars, which would carry them as far as Winnipeg or British Columbia. A transatlantic liner might require two to three trains to carry all the passengers and their baggage heading west. The operation was hugely efficient.

So it was a sad state of affairs that Pier 27 which had celebrated the arrival of so many new immigrants into Canada — some three million men and women over its long history — was now being used as the temporary morgue for the hundreds of victims of the *Empress* disaster.

In the rain, a silent column of people, young and old, filed slowly along Pier 27 towards the purple drapes covering the entrance. Alice and Pauline stepped around the rain puddles and passed through the purple drapes. Inside the darkened hall, the bodies lay in cheap pine boxes on tables covered in black crepe. When space ran out on the tables, the caskets were placed on the ground. Candles illuminated the faces of the dead and the mourners as they filed past. The hall echoed with the cries of distressed family members. The adults lined the tables along the walls with the children in child-size coffins in the centre.

Many of the bodies were grotesquely disfigured, and the smell of death was overpowering. Pauline held a handkerchief to her nose as she led Alice down the row of dead children. Alice stopped suddenly.

"Oh, my God!" she recoiled in horror. "Jamie, is that you?"

Pauline turned and stared in shock as Alice threw herself on the lifeless body of a little boy in a sailor suit. His face was horribly disfigured, smashed by debris from the ship and tumefied from a long immersion in the river.

"It's my Jamie!" Alice sobbed. "Jamie, what has happened to you?"

Pauline tried to comfort Alice when a police constable came over to talk to them.

"You are the family?" he asked in heavily accented English.

"*C'est la mère du petit, monsieur,*" Pauline said.

The constable looked sadly at Alice, then stepped closer to Pauline and lowered his voice.

"*Il y a une femme qui a reclamé le corps il y a moins d'une heure.*"

"*Ce n'est pas possible!*" Pauline exclaimed.

She realized that Alice had overheard the constable and was trying to understand what the man had said.

"The constable informed me," Pauline said, "that the child has been claimed already."

Alice seized the boy's hand and glared at the policeman.
"This is my child!" Alice shouted. "This is my Jamie."
"*Oui, madame,*" the constable replied, anxious to avoid any further argument.
"Don't worry, Alice," Pauline said, "we'll work this out."

There was tension in the smoking room of the *Château Frontenac* as the two men faced off.
"Kendall is quite unreliable, sir," Walters declared.
"I cannot agree," said Butler Aspinall, the smartly dressed London solicitor with a waxed moustache. "I think he'll testify coherently. After all, he's a company man and the captain of the ship. How long has he been with us?"
"Eleven years," Walters said. "You don't know him. He could break at any time."
Sir Thomas Shea was a railroad builder and president of CPR operations in Canada. He sat in a green leather armchair puffing on a cigar and weighing the opinions of the two men before him. He had not yet invited either man to sit down.
"Do you gentlemen realize the risks involved here?" Shea asked. "Already ticket sales are down on the *Empress of Britain*, which left Liverpool a week Tuesday. There's gossip going around that CP ships are unsafe."
Shea held up a telegram.
"See this. It says the *Empress of India* sailed from Hong Kong to Vancouver with only half its usual complement of passengers. Sales are down on all CP ships, gentlemen. White Star and Allan ships are carrying twice what we carry. We're losing money. So tell me, can he bloody well testify or can't he?"
"I had a talk with him, sir," Aspinall said. "I think he can

testify."

"He's a serious danger to our case," Walters claimed. "I don't think he will hold up in court."

"He's the captain, sir," Aspinall said. "There is no way around him. We cannot keep him from testifying."

Shea angrily stubbed out his cigar in the ashtray.

"We cannot take a chance on this man losing control and making a laughing stock of us all. Gentlemen, millions of pounds are at stake all because of that bloody collier from nowhere. Do you understand the gravity of the situation?"

In the warm June sunshine, Godefroy sat with his hand on the tiller of the *Rose des Vents* working the debris field. The wind was up and the water was choppy, making their work more difficult. Young Thomas was in the bow with the gaff, observing the green iridescent waters of the St. Lawrence while Louis stood near the main sail searching for bodies with binoculars. They approached a mass of floating debris, including some wooden barrels and planks. Thomas prodded the debris with the gaff.

"Nothing, *Père*."

Godefroy swung the boat around, tacking towards the shore.

"Let's go in. I think we're too far out."

The debris field from the ship had now spread east over a large area from Rimouski to Matane, some sixty miles downstream.

Godefroy and his sons had just pulled another floater from the river and were leaving the area when Thomas spotted something on the horizon.

"There's something floating over there, *Père*."

"What is it?"

"I don't know. It looks like more debris," Thomas said, observing the horizon.

Godefroy turned the boat, and they sailed towards the floating debris.

"There's a man on it," Louis remarked, astonished.

"That can't be," Thomas said.

"Yes, it's a man, and he's moving. He's alive, *Père*."

"That's not possible," Godefroy added. "You must be mistaken, Louis."

Twelve

At the Mount Hermon cemetery in Quebec City, a crowd had gathered near the graves of a dozen victims of the *Empress* disaster. Several horse-drawn hearses were parked near the well-wishers. A priest said a prayer as he walked along the line of coffins near the gravesite. An honour guard of soldiers from the Royal 22nd Regiment was present. Among the crowd of onlookers, there was Captain Kendall, accompanied by First Officer Johnson.

As the service came to an end and the people dispersed, Kendall and Johnson took a *calèche* or calash, a light four-wheeled carriage with a folding top, back to town. They stopped in the Plains of Abraham Park to walk along a path overlooking the river. Kendall was limping, leaning heavily on his cane.

"So what did Walters have to say?" Johnson asked.

"We talked about the inquiry. They're worried about my testimony."

"Sir, I don't think I need to tell you this, but there is no better time to make the bastards sing."

Kendall stopped, looking annoyed.

"What are they offering you?" Johnson asked.

Kendall stumbled on, ignoring the question.

"Don't be foolish, Henry," Johnson snapped. "Your

testimony can sink or save the case for them. You, me and Murphy are the only surviving witnesses who were on the bridge."

Kendall turned back to Johnson, his face flushed with rage.

"What the hell were you doing that night?" Kendall asked.

Johnson smirked at the captain.

"You mean when I left the bridge?"

Kendall nodded.

"Would it help you to know?" Johnson asked. "I was collecting a bet."

"You know the trouble you caused us."

"Oh, no. Don't you go blaming me, Henry. You could have run to the north shore to avoid the damn fog. That's what I would have done. I would have given that fucking collier a wide berth. Instead, you put yourself on a collision course with the bloody ship."

Kendall turned and walked on.

"Henry, I am with you on this," Johnson pleaded. "I have to know what they are offering you."

As the *Rose des Vents* approached the floating debris, it became clear that the man was not moving. He was lying on a makeshift raft made from a wooden flat lashed to an inner tube and several cork life jackets. Louis had mistaken the movement of the raft on the waves for the movements of the man himself.

When they got close, Thomas used the gaff to pull the raft alongside the boat. The man was either dead or unconscious. Godefroy leaned over the gunwale to see if he was breathing. After a moment, he looked back at his sons.

"*Il est vivant*. He's alive!" he shouted, incredulous.

It had been more than sixty hours since the *Empress* had

gone down.

"Help me pull him in. Louis, take his legs," Godefroy ordered.

With Thomas holding on to the raft, Louis and Godefroy pulled the man on board.

"Thomas, get me some water right quick."

"He's been out here a long time," Louis remarked.

Thomas ran off and returned with a water bottle. Godefroy managed to pour some water down the throat of the man. He woke up coughing and suddenly took fright.

"What's your name, sir?" Godefroy asked.

The man looked around at Godefroy and his sons in a state of high agitation before he fainted.

Charles Haight, the elegantly dressed lawyer from New York, looked somewhat out of place in the *Storstad* mess room. In a pinstripe frock coat with a carefully clipped goatee and mutton chops, he looked more like a college professor than a practising solicitor working in the Admiralty courts. As guest of honour, he was seated at the head table next to Captain Andersen, John Griffin, First Officer Toftenes, and Third Officer Saxe facing the crew sitting around the room.

"I called this meeting so Mr Haight would have the opportunity to meet with you before the inquiry begins," Griffin said. "He just arrived by train from New York this morning and I have been getting him up to date. Perhaps, Mr Haight, you would like to say a word or two to the men."

Haight picked up his glass of aquavit and downed it. His dark eyes brightened as he looked at the hard group of men - the engine-room crew in greasy blue coveralls and the deckhands in ragged clothing - with the pervasive smell of tobacco and sweat lingering in the air. A child's teddy bear with a red ribbon around the neck sat on a table near a huge mountain of a man named Thor.

"Thank you, John. I'm very happy to have arrived and I will do my best to defend your interests during the inquiry. Most of my career has been spent working on cases involving shipping accidents of various kinds on the East coast."

Frida appeared at the table with a bottle and refilled the glasses with aquavit.

"Thank you. It's very good. Is it Norwegian?" Haight asked.

"Yes, sir," Frida said. "It comes from my village in Norway."

"You are men from the West coast of Norway, I believe."

"Yes, most of the crew is from Bergen except for Fremmerlid, who comes from way up north," Andersen said.

The men grinned at Fremmerlid, and laughter was heard.

"So you are in North America for the work?" Haight asked.

"Yes, we work the North Sea, the Baltic, and we follow the work here," Andersen said.

Toftenes, a handsome young man with a large moustache and thinning blond hair, seemed eager to catch Haight's eye.

"Mr Haight, how long do you think this inquiry will take?"

"You are?" Haight asked the young officer.

Griffin whispered in his ear.

"Ah, Mr Toftenes. I read your statement coming up on the train. You are the first officer?"

"Yes, sir," Toftenes said.

"It should take a few weeks at the most."

"There's been a lot of bad press, Mr Haight," Andersen added. "What do you think are our chances?"

"Well, I wouldn't really know at this stage," Haight said. "You are in America. You'll get a fair shake."

"I think this is not America," Toftenes said. "This Lord Mersey, he is British. I do not trust this man."

"Well, I believe he'll be fair. He came down very hard on Captain Smith of the *Titanic*. He won't stand for any nonsense."

Fremmerlid stood up and laid a bronze plaque inscribed with the number 328 on the table.

"Fremmerlid found this on the bridge after the collision," Andersen said.

"Yes, I mentioned it to Mr Haight," Griffin added.

"It's quite amazing," Haight said as he examined the plaque.

"It must have fallen off during impact," Andersen said.

"This could be important," Haight said. "You must take care not to lose it. We might need to produce it during the inquiry."

He looked around the room at the silent men. There was the undeniable smell of fear among them. The crew had never been involved in such a high-stakes incident and there was genuine unease in the room. It was obvious to Haight that the lives of these men would be on hold until the end of the inquiry. The *Storstad* and its men were not going anywhere as they awaited the outcome.

Thirteen

'We have been so worried about you. The news in the papers here has been devastating. So many victims. Everyone blames the Norwegians and expresses the greatest sympathy for you. I think of you every day, my darling.'

Kendall looked wistfully out the window of his room at the *Château Frontenac*, then returned to his wife's letter.

'Tim got such good marks at school that his master chose him to read a poem in front of the whole school. He chose Kipling. I am so proud of him as you will be.'

Kendall imagined his small son in a prep school jacket and tie nervously reciting a poem in front of a large assembly of English schoolboys. In his mind's eye, Kendall could hear his son's hesitant voice as he read Kipling's famous poem 'If':

"*If you can keep your head when all about you*
Are losing theirs and blaming it on you;
If you can trust yourself when all men doubt you,
But make allowance for their doubting too;
If you can wait and not be tired by waiting,
Or being lied about, don't deal in lies,
Or being hated, don't give way to hating,
And yet don't look too good, nor talk too wise."

Kendall had stopped reading and was reciting the poem by

heart as he watched the ships in the harbour coming and going.

"You still here, Mr Ashby?" Peters asked as the insurance investigator entered the CPR office.

"Yes, sir. I still have work to do in the city."

Ashby put on his spectacles to read the name on the document he was holding.

"I'm looking for a second-class passenger by the name of Alan Burke," Ashby said. "He was on your list of survivors in Rimouski but now seems to have disappeared."

"He's probably gone home, sir."

"Yes, that is what I thought at first, but his family thinks he might be dead. They have had no news from their prodigal son. He comes from a silver mining family in Colorado and they have a sizeable claim on his life."

"Wouldn't you need a body to collect on a life insurance policy, sir?" Peters asked.

"Under normal circumstances, you would."

"I don't understand, Mr Ashby. You said that he was marked as a survivor on our list in Rimouski."

"That's why I flagged the case, Mr Peters. He has made no attempt to contact his family. They are sending someone who can identify the body."

"Could this man in Rimouski have been someone else trying to catch a free ride to Quebec?"

"That's quite possible. He could have consulted the passenger list, which was readily available, and decided to use that name to claim free passage on the train. Or, he could be the real Alan Burke and is now trying to claim on his family's policy by disappearing."

Peters looked puzzled.

"You wouldn't remember the man from the train station, would you, Mr Peters?" Ashby said. "You were there."

"Yes, I was, but I can't remember seeing this man. We were so busy that day."

"*Hey, Godefroy. Comment ça va?* Any new cadavers?"

Bob was standing at the bar in a Rimouski hotel as Godefroy entered the establishment in the middle of the day. His eyes took some time to adjust to the dim light before he noticed Bob waving him over. The bar had a rustic look with its deer antlers and stuffed moose heads on the knotty pine wall panels.

"*Bonjour, Bob,*" he said.

"You chaps brought in over forty cadavers," Bob said with pride. "You beat out everyone else!"

Bob was a CPR fixer who had been hastily assigned the task of organizing the local fishermen in a hunt for *Empress* cadavers. He wore city clothes and sported a patchy goatee under an alky nose.

"A drink for my friend here?" he shouted to the barman.

"Thanks, Bob," Godefroy said. "We are lucky, you know. We were one of the first boats out there with the *Lady Evelyn* and the *Eureka*. I never want to see anything like that again, dead people floating on the water."

"Well, it was good work while it lasted. I'm returning to Quebec at the end of the week."

A whisky arrived with a refresher for Bob. Godefroy took a slug and put down his glass.

"I got a bit of a problem, Bob," Godefroy said, wiping his moustache on his sleeve. "We found a live passenger out on the river."

Bob looked flabbergasted.

"A live one. You're joking, right?"

"No, sir. It's no joke."

"I don't fucking believe it."

"It's true. I don't make a joke, Bob."

"I only pay for the dead, Godefroy. What the hell am I supposed to do with a live one?"

Godefroy looked at Bob and sipped his whisky.

"Man or woman?" Bob asked.

"A young man, I think a foreigner. Dr Morin is going to examine him."

"How much do you want for a live one?"

"I don't know," Godefroy said. "He must be worth more than a dead one."

"They're gonna think I'm aiding and abetting a fuckin' ambulance chaser. A live one, you say. They ain't gonna believe it. You better take it to the CPR yourself, old chum."

"It's from your sister Agnes," Andersen said.

Frida wiped her hands on her apron before taking the telegram and ripping it open. Andersen watched her impatiently, standing near a pot of soup in the *Storstad* ship's galley.

"What does it say?" he asked.

"She writes: 'Saw your picture in the news. I'm in Chicago on my way east. Will arrive in Quebec June 18 with Niels.' She's coming east to see us."

"What about the husband?"

"No mention of the husband," Frida said. "Maybe it's just a brief visit."

"I don't understand, Frida. Her husband is a farmer, and he's probably busy seeding this time of year. This is no time to leave the farm."

"Well, she's on her way here."

Frida was ecstatic with the news and couldn't care less about the husband and the farm. Her sister was coming for a visit. That was all she needed to know. She kissed her husband before running out of the galley to their cabin.

Fourteen

"Lord Mersey?"

Ezekiel McLeod and Sir Adolphe-Basile Routhier had just arrived at the bar of the *Château Frontenac* to greet the famous British jurist. And there he was, drinking a whisky in the dark interior.

"Gentlemen," Lord Mersey said, stepping off the barstool.

John Charles Bigham QC, Viscount Mersey, was a dour, no-nonsense British jurist and politician, clean-shaven with a receding hairline. He had been appointed commissioner in charge of the *Titanic* Inquiry and had just arrived by ship from Liverpool.

"We have been expecting you, sir. I am Adolphe-Basile Routhier and this is my colleague, Ezekiel McLeod."

Lord Mersey shook hands with his visitors, who smiled warmly at their celebrated visitor. Routhier was a francophone and had retired as Chief Justice of the Quebec Superior Court in 1906. He was a writer, university professor and well-known orator in French Canada. He had written the original French lyrics of "O Canada", the Canadian national anthem, in his early years on the bench and had been knighted in 1911. He was an ultramontanist, who believed in papal infallibility and the primacy of the Church over the State, and was therefore very conservative in his views. He was short and slim with a bushy moustache and mutton chops.

McLeod was Chief Justice of New Brunswick and had been a lawyer, judge and political figure in the province. While Routhier had a friendly, easy-going manner, McLeod was a rather stern Scot who tended to be distrustful and judgmental.

"I just got in an hour ago," Lord Mersey said.

"How was the crossing, sir?" McLeod asked.

"It was perfectly horrible. I was sick as a dog for most of the week. I was just getting my sea legs when we arrived in the St. Lawrence."

"Sorry to hear that, sir," Routhier said.

"Let me get you some drinks and then you gentlemen can tell me what you have planned."

Lord Mersey raised his hand to call over the barman.

Alice and Vicky sat at one end of the long table silently picking at their food as several scruffy young men, lodgers at the rooming house, finished their meal. Pauline came in from the kitchen as the cook cleared the plates away. She sat down near Alice and Vicky.

"You must eat more than that, my dear," Pauline said. "What will your parents think?"

She stopped talking when she realized her mistake. Alice glanced angrily at her.

"I don't care," Vicky said, getting up and hugging Alice before running up the stairs to her bedroom.

Pauline and Alice watched her go.

"I think it's time you told the child the truth."

"I think you're right," Alice murmured.

"You've done all you can."

Alice nodded.

"Have you had any news from her family?" Pauline asked.

"No, nothing. I suppose the authorities have been too busy to contact the next of kin."

"I'll make some inquiries if you like."

"Gentlemen, I fear you have been misinformed. I know absolutely nothing about maritime affairs," Lord Mersey said, slurring his words.

The fatigue of the voyage and the drinks were having their effect on the English gentleman. They were finishing the main course in the dining room of the *Château Frontenac*. Several waiters hovered nearby, filling their glasses with abundant quantities of French wines.

"My knowledge of the law is limited to railways, canals, and bankruptcy in that order. Commercial law is my bailiwick and I am counting on you two gentlemen to help me sort out the issues in this case."

Judges Routhier and McLeod were astonished. Routhier recovered first.

"My colleague here is well versed in Canadian maritime law," Routhier said, "as he hails from New Brunswick, but I really know very little or nothing about cases like this."

"I'm not sure about that," McLeod said. "I have not been involved in that many cases."

"Your reputation precedes you, sir," Routhier said to Lord Mersey. "I think you are being very modest, understating the importance of your work on the *Titanic* Inquiry."

"That case wasn't so hard, you know," Lord Mersey said. "A freak accident, a passenger liner colliding with an iceberg. Excessive speed was the principal cause."

"I have read reports that Captain Smith and the White Star

line got off too easy," McLeod said.

"Of course they did. Every bloody sea captain and shipping company on the New York route has been pushing for faster passage times, so there was nothing exceptional in what Smith did. They were going too fast, they were careless."

Lord Mersey took a sip of wine before continuing.

"The inquiry went on far too long with testimony from a hundred witnesses. It lasted 36 tedious days. We can do a lot better this time around, don't you think? We should be able to wrap it up in two weeks."

"Two weeks?" McLeod asked, astonished.

"Stick to the facts of the case, that's my advice. It should be relatively simple. Which of the two ships is to blame? What do you think?"

"I've read the statements of both sides, sir," Routhier said. "It's not at all clear who is to blame."

"Well, I'm sure with your help we'll soon find our guilty party," Lord Mersey said.

"You've heard about the *Helvetia* sinking?" McLeod asked.

"No, I don't think I have."

"Well, sir, the sister ship, the *Empress of Britain*, ran into a collier in a fog on the river not two years ago. It sank the *Helvetia* but managed to save the crew. No lives were lost. The circumstances were very similar."

"The master of the ship was Captain Murray," Routhier added. "He's the harbour master here in Quebec now. He was the master of the *Empress of Ireland*, sir, until very recently."

"So what was the conclusion of the investigation?" Lord Mersey asked. "There must have been an inquiry."

"Murray was found guilty of excessive speed, sir. The *Helvetia* was stopped in the water," McLeod said.

"Well, well. Excessive speed seems to be the root cause of a lot of these maritime accidents," Lord Mersey said.

"Captain Murray was lucky not to lose his master's certificate, sir," McLeod said. "The judges thought he did an admirable job saving the lives of the *Helvetia* crew."

"Will this case have any influence on the present one?" Lord Mersey asked.

"I doubt it, sir," McLeod said, "but it does go to show the frequency of these accidents on the river when there's a fog."

"By the way, has your minister put together a list of questions for the inquiry?" Lord Mersey asked. "I requested this in my acceptance telegram."

"Yes, sir. It arrived yesterday," McLeod confirmed.

Alice entered the bedroom to find Vicky lying on her bed playing with a music box. She wound it up and then opened the lid, watching the miniature dancer whirling around to the tinny sound of Tchaikovsky's Nutcracker Suite.

Alice sat down and stroked Vicky's hair.

"See how she goes around and around, Alice."

"Yes, dear."

The music finally came to an end as the dancer stopped moving. Vicky closed the lid and looked up at Alice.

"My mum and dad are not coming back?"

"No, dear. They're not coming back. I'm so sorry."

"Can I stay with you, Alice? You'll be my mummy."

Alice looked stunned as she observed the joyful expression on the child's face.

"You smell like her," Vicky said, cajoling Alice and squeezing her arm. "You talk like her."

"Do I now?" Alice asked.

"Yes, you do. You have the same voice."

"The same voice?" Alice whispered as her eyes filled with tears. She was thinking about her lost husband and son.

"You cry like her too," Vicky said, putting her arm around Alice.

"Stop it, Vicky, please."

Vicky stepped away and collected her dolly, cradling it in her arms.

"No one can ever replace your mother, Vicky. She'll always be your mum."

Fifteen

"Frida!" Agnes Evensen shouted as she descended from the train in the crowded CPR train station with her six-year-old son Niels.

"*Hei*, Agnes!"

Frida rushed forward to embrace her younger sister, followed by Alfred Toftenes. The two women were both fair-haired and had the same distinctive traits, but Agnes was the prettier of the two. Frida turned to little Niels and swept him up in her arms.

"Niels, this is your Auntie Frida," Agnes said.

"Hello, Niels."

"Hello, Auntie," Niels replied.

Niels looked nervously at Frida and then at Alfred.

"We're so happy to finally arrive," Agnes said. "Aren't we, Niels?"

Niels took his mother's hand but remained silent.

"*Hei*, Alfred. I remember you."

"*Velkommen*, Agnes."

Toftenes collected Agnes' suitcase and followed the women as they walked arm-in-arm along the platform with Niels.

"Niels likes trains," Agnes said.

"I'm sure he does," Frida said, smiling at the boy.

SHIPWRECKED LIVES

In the late afternoon, a wagon descended a rutted track through the woods of *Anse-aux-Coques* towards the Paradis farm. Godefroy, in a flat cap and scarf, held the reins, sitting next to the elderly Dr Morin in a bowler hat. The sun was low in the sky as they pulled into the Paradis yard and climbed down. Through the kitchen window, the children watched them arrive, entering the house through the summer kitchen.

Justine looked up as they appeared on the doorstep.

"Bonjour, Dr Morin."

Morin tipped his bowler hat in response.

"*Comment il va?*" Godefroy asked his wife.

"He's sleeping," Justine said.

Morin nodded as he removed his hat, revealing his hairless skull. He was a man of few words, kind-hearted but with a gruff exterior. He took out a pair of spectacles and put them on just as young Françoise stepped into the room.

"Bonjour, Dr Morin. His name is Simo, *Père*."

"Is he talking?" Godefroy asked.

"Not much and none in French or English."

"Then how do you know his name?"

"He wrote it down. We're talking in signs, *Père*."

Godefroy was not surprised by his daughter's progress communicating with this strange man. Françoise was a quick study for her age. She led them into the small downstairs bedroom where Simo was fast asleep.

As Dr Morin approached the bed, Simo awakened with a start. His arm had a nasty gash on it that had been treated by Justine with a poultice to draw out the infection. The doctor examined his arm.

"What do we have here?"

"The cut was infected, *Maman* made the poultice," Françoise said.

"Nicely done."

As Morin examined the arm, Françoise showed him the name of the man written on a scrap of paper.

"Mr Simo, then. How are you feeling?" Morin asked.

Simo shook his head, incapable of comprehending the question.

"Can you stand up?"

Simo frowned as Godefroy helped him to his feet.

"Very good, sir," Dr Morin said. "Let's see you walk now?"

Simo seemed to understand and stumbled clumsily around the room.

"Sit down, please."

Françoise made a sign with her hand, indicating that the doctor wanted Simo to sit. He sat down on the edge of the bed and the doctor examined his eyes and throat.

"Off with the shirt, please."

Françoise made a sign for Simo to remove his shirt. Godefroy took the shirt as the doctor started to auscultate his lungs with a stethoscope.

"So when are we going home, *Mamma*?" Niels asked.

Agnes had put the boy to bed in the captain's cabin after reading him a story.

"Do you miss your *pappa*?" Agnes asked Niels.

"No, never. I hate Olaf. I want to go sailing with Auntie Frida and the captain."

"I do too, Niels. I do too. Sleep tight, darling."

Agnes kissed the boy.

"Are you scared of *pappa*?" Niels asked.

"Not anymore, now that we're with Auntie Frida, we'll be

fine."

"Will *pappa* come after us?"

"He may try, but we'll never go back. Good night, my love. Sweet dreams."

"Good night, *Mamma*."

Agnes stood up and blew out the oil lamp on the desk. She left the room, pulling the door half closed because Niels was afraid of the dark. She joined Frida in the mess room with the remains of the evening meal. The captain and the crew were off, having a drink in town. Frida poured Agnes a cup of tea and then sat down near her quietly.

"How is Niels?"

"Fine."

"He's such a lovely boy, Agnes."

"He takes after his father, of course," Agnes said. "Olaf is a handsome man."

"So tell me the whole story, Agnes."

"You remember Olaf when we lived in Norway."

"Yes, I do. He was quite intense, if I remember correctly."

"Yes, he was a very serious young man when I first met him. I should have seen the signs."

"A lot of young men were like him in our village, Agnes. Lots of serious boys turn out well."

"You remember his parents. His dad was such a stern, unforgiving man. He beat Olaf black and blue when he was just a young child."

"Yes, I remember something about the family. Spare the rod and spoil the child. A lot of children were brought up harshly in our village."

"I know, but I thought Olaf would be different. I was in love with him when I went to America. He was good to me that first year when we bought the farm in Minnesota and started working it. Then the soybean crop failed. We had no rain for months. It was so dry and hot that summer. That's when things went from bad to worse. During the winter Olaf spent all our money on feed for the livestock. That was the winter Niels was born. We had nothing but the clothes on our backs and it was so cold."

"I remember you wrote me that winter," Frida said.

"We had our dreams. How we would make a lot of money with our crops. Olaf comes from a farming family, but he's not a good farmer. He's too impatient, too ready to spend money. The second year we had a good harvest, but the price of soybeans had dropped and we barely made enough to pull through."

Frida poured two glasses of aquavit, one for herself and one for Agnes. She handed a glass to her sister.

"The third year Olaf started going crazy. He would beat me up for nothing. I had to help him in the fields during the day, do the cooking, look after Niels and clean the house. I was exhausted, but it was never enough for Olaf. He got it into his head that I was undermining his work. When something went wrong, I was to blame. I had done something bad on purpose."

"So you saw our picture in the paper?"

"Yes, it was in the local newspaper in town, a picture of the *Storstad*," Agnes said. "I couldn't believe it, your ship was in a collision with a passenger liner. I remembered the name from your letters. It was then that I knew Niels and I must leave. We knew you would be in Quebec for some time."

"How did you get away?"

"It wasn't easy, Frida. We escaped in the middle of the night after Olaf fell asleep. I had saddled the horse beforehand and hidden my bag in the barn. I woke Niels in the early morning hours and dressed him. Then we took the horse into town where we caught the train to Chicago. I had some savings from the money Olaf gave me for provisions, so we had just enough for the fare to Quebec."

Sixteen

"My Lord, the commission has been read and the purpose of the inquiry has been made known. It is a commission constituted under statutory powers to investigate the causes of a shipping casualty, which has caused a most dreadful loss of life."

Crown counsel Newcombe read his speech from a podium in the Quebec City courtroom on St. Louis Street in the old town. Behind the massive bench sat Lord Mersey flanked by the Canadian judges Routhier and McLeod. In front of them, sitting at low tables on either side of the aisle, were Butler Aspinall and the CPR defence counsellors on one side and Charles Haight and the *Storstad* defence counsellors on the other. The courtroom was packed with reporters from around the world. There was barely enough standing room along the walls.

"The steamship *Empress of Ireland* left Quebec at twenty-seven minutes past four on the afternoon of the 28th of May with 1477 persons on board on her way to Liverpool," Newcombe said. "During the night, after leaving her pilot off Cock Point buoy near Father Point on the south shore of the St. Lawrence River, she came into collision with the Norwegian steamer *Storstad* bound for Montreal from Sydney, Nova Scotia with a full cargo of coal. The catastrophe was very sudden. The *Empress* received a very severe blow to her starboard or right side. She began to fill, turned over on her beam ends and sank almost immediately. The loss of life was colossal. 1,014 passengers and crew lost their lives while 463 were saved."

"Who is this American lawyer Haight?" Lord Mersey asked his colleagues Routhier and McLeod.

They were seated in the dining room of the *Château Frontenac* during the lunch break. The room was full, and the waiters struggled to serve a copious meal on silver platters to their illustrious guests.

"Charles S. Haight has quite the reputation in New York, sir," McLeod said. "The firm of Haight, Gardner, Poor and Havens is well established in the practice of maritime law on this side of the Atlantic. They have a long history of litigation in maritime affairs."

Mersey looked unconvinced as he drank his wine.

"Haight's an expert in maritime affairs," Routhier added.

"Good for him. He's going to need it, I think, against a barrister like Butler Aspinall K.C. whom I worked with on the *Titanic* case. Aspinall's very shrewd and knowledgeable. I expect this case will be quite challenging for Mr Haight."

"The CPR has launched a motion in Admiralty court to seize the *Storstad* for damages, sir," Routhier said.

Lord Mersey looked sceptical.

"Isn't that a little premature?"

"Seizing the asset, I don't think so," McLeod said. "The aim is simply to prevent the ship from leaving Canadian waters."

"But the ship is damaged. It isn't going anywhere," Lord Mersey said.

"It's a show of force, sir," Routhier said.

"It's a sly move," McLeod added. "It's a way of showing how untrustworthy the Norwegians are. Shea wants his pound of flesh."

"He was five years old," Alice said. "His birthday was a month ago."

Inspector Mainguy, a heavyset man with bushy eyebrows and a closely clipped moustache, was sitting at his desk, opening a file on the missing child. He wrote Alice's name at the top of the sheet with a blue fountain pen.

Alice looked around the office with its antique wooden desk piled high with files and the beat-up filing cabinet in the corner near the coat rack. Her attention was drawn to the photograph on the wall of the popular mayor of the city, Olivier-Napoléon Drouin, who had won re-election in 1912 on an austerity platform. The city had been in economic decline for over a decade and the police department was running on empty. They had been struggling with reduced staff even before the *Empress* disaster had occurred.

The economic downturn had started with the decline in wooden shipbuilding along the shore of the St. Lawrence and was exacerbated by the lack of a rail link to the south shore. The collapse of the Quebec Bridge during construction in 1907 hadn't helped the situation.

"Weight and height, please."

"I'm not sure," Alice said, raising her hand to estimate the height of the boy, "about this high, maybe three and a half feet, about 40 pounds."

"Eyes, hair?"

"Blue eyes like his father, brown hair."

"What about pictures? Any snapshots of the boy that could help us identify him?" Mainguy asked.

"I lost everything on the ship, sir."

"Of course."

Alice suddenly broke down and started to cry.

"I know this is painful for you, Mrs Bingham."

Alice nodded as she wiped the tears from her eyes and tried to concentrate on the inspector's questions.

"What about birthmarks, scars?"

"Yes, he has a birthmark on his arm, the right arm near the elbow."

"Anything else? Is the boy circumcised?"

"Yes, he is."

"Well then, that's about it for the time being. You need to sign here."

Inspector Mainguy turned the register towards Alice, who picked up the pen and signed at the bottom.

"The birthmark should do, shouldn't it?" Alice asked.

"I have no idea," Mainguy said, "I still haven't received the coroner's report."

"Who are these people who claim my Jamie?"

"The Thompsons are a well-respected family. They are convinced the child is theirs."

"That's impossible. There can be no doubt."

"We're just doing our jobs, *madame*. There are so many bodies needing identification. I'll contact you again in a few days."

Alice stood up and shook the inspector's hand before heading for the door. As she left city hall, she ran into James Galt in the old town.

"Hello, Miss Bingham. How are you and young Vicky getting along?"

Alice tried to smile at James but finally looked away.

"Are you sure you're all right?"

"I'm sorry, Mr Galt," Alice said, wiping a tear from her eye. "I just had a rather disturbing meeting with a police inspector."

"Well, I think I know the perfect remedy. Come on, Miss Alice. There's a German bakery around the corner. They have the most marvellous apple strudel."

Alice laughed at this.

"You're looking a bit pale. The food will do you good."

"Thank you, James."

She took his arm, and they headed off together.

NAVIGATION LIGHTS
(VESSELS UNDERWAY)

BOW VIEW

STERN VIEW

PORT VIEW

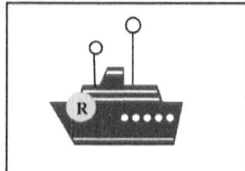

STARBOARD VIEW

Seventeen

Captain Kendall looked alert and unruffled, as he stood in the witness box in his captain's uniform taking questions from the Butler Aspinall. His weathered face with its strong jawline gave him an undeniable air of authority before the court.

"Captain Kendall, do you not hold an extra Master's certificate?" Aspinall asked.

"Yes."

"How long have you had it?"

"12 years."

"How long have you been in the service of the Canadian Pacific Steamship Company?"

"Eleven and a half years."

"And on the night of the casualty were you the master of the *Empress of Ireland*?"

"I was."

"Now, on the night of the disaster, you dropped your pilot at Father Point?"

"About a mile north of the Father Point gas buoy on the steamer Eureka."

"After having dropped your pilot, what was your course?"

"North 50 degrees east by compass," Kendall said, remembering the events of that fateful night.

It was a clear night as the Empress left Father Point and headed out into the river. In the wheelhouse, Quartermaster Murphy was at the helm as First Officer Johnson used the telegraph to give an order to the engine-room. A signal of one bell was heard from the crow's nest indicating a vessel approaching on the horizon. With his binoculars, Kendall sighted a steamer six miles off on their starboard beam (right side).

"Port the helm, Johnson, north 76 degrees east. I am going up to check the compass."

"Yes, sir. North 76 degrees east," Johnson ordered.

Kendall climbed the ladder to the upper bridge to check the heading on the magnetic compass while the Third Officer Moore, the quartermasters Murphy and Sharples, and a messenger boy stood by.

"When we got the signal from Carroll in the crow's nest," Kendall said. "I could see the two masthead lights of the *Storstad*."

"The *Storstad* was carrying two masthead lights?" Aspinall asked.

"Yes, I could see the main masthead light, which is higher than the forward light. The lights were open."

"So you could see a coloured light?"

"No, all I could see were the masthead lights which were open on her starboard side."

"So you saw the lower forward masthead light to your right and the higher main masthead light to your left, which told you that she was showing her starboard side, her right side?"

"Yes."

"Was the weather clear?" Aspinall asked.

"Yes."

"Was there any risk of collision at that distance?"

"No."

"So you saw that the masthead lights of the *Storstad* were open in such a way that it told you as a sailor that she was starboard to your starboard and going for a left-hand passage?"

"It did. Then I went up to the navigation bridge to check the standard compass."

"Who was in charge during your absence?"

"It only takes a moment to go up. Of course, First Officer Johnson was in charge."

"What happened when you returned?"

"I noticed a fog bank spreading out from the land and it started to get misty."

"By this time had you seen anything other than the masthead lights?"

"When I came down from the navigation bridge, I saw their green or starboard light."

"And the fog was beginning to dim her lights?"

"Yes."

"Outside of the fog bank, are you and the *Storstad* coming up starboard to starboard."

"Absolutely."

"Seeing this fog bank travelling out from land towards your ship and the other ship, did you do anything?"

"I did."

"What did you do?"

"When I saw their lights were getting misty, I stopped my ship."

"Did you blow an appropriate signal whistle when you did that?"

"I did."

"What whistle did you give?"

"Three short blasts."

"What effect had the stopping and reversing of your engines?" Aspinall asked. "Did it take your way off?"

"It did."

"How did you ascertain whether your way was off or not?"

"By looking over the side of the ship."

"What information did you gather from that?"

"By the foam and air bubbles on the water."

"Is it a common practice for seamen to look over the side in a fog to see whether their ship is stopped?"

"It is."

"Before you looked over the side, had you blown another set of three blasts?"

"Yes, I did it before the way was off the ship."

Charles Haight raised his eyebrows and locked eyes with his colleague John Griffin. Clearly, Kendall's decision to stop his ship as soon as the fog came up was a weak point in the CPR defence. But the captain was putting on a good show and it would not be easy to shake the court's confidence in his testimony.

"I was an English teacher until I had Jamie," Alice said as she tucked into her apple strudel.

Alice and James were sitting at a corner table in a German cafe, drinking tea and eating homemade pastries.

"I taught English in the schools in Toronto. English literature was my specialty."

"Shakespeare?" James asked.

"Yes, of course. Dickens, Austen, Hardy, Wilde, Eliot, a lot of authors. We introduce our pupils to a wide range of literature."

"I was never much good at school, Alice. I don't know any of those names. On the ship, we'd sometimes get penny dreadfuls and magazines, you know. Some of the stories weren't so bad. On my last trip, I found a copy of *The Sign of the Four* in the first-class dining room. It had that Sherlock detective chap and his partner Dr Watson in it. They're trying to solve a mystery about some pearls arriving in the mail. I was quite taken with it. Do you know it?"

"Arthur Conan Doyle."

"Yes, that's him. So you must know the story."

"I like Doyle, but he's not on our approved list."

James drank his tea and smiled at Alice with her prim and proper air of the schoolmarm.

"You'll return to teaching when you go home, Alice?"

"Yes, I suppose I will. I love working with children."

James pulled a piece of writing paper from a pocket.

"My mates have asked me to write a letter to the mother of our third officer, Charles Moore. He was always very nice to the crew. He drowned after his lifeboat crashed into the river."

James pushed the ink-stained paper across to Alice, who picked it up and started to read.

"I thought you might take a look at it."

Alice read the brief missive in its scratchy handwriting and crossed out words and then smiled warmly at James.

"I like the part where you say how nice your friend Charles was and how much his shipmates liked him."

"He really was a very good chap. We'll miss him."

"I'm sure you will, James," Alice said in a reserved tone, "but you certainly can't say 'I know how you feel' in a condolence letter. That won't do."

"I can't say that?" James asked.

"No, James, you cannot presume to know how his mother feels, no one can."

The schoolmarm was gone. Alice smiled, looking very pale and fragile like a china doll.

Eighteen

"It takes about two minutes to stop the ship," Kendall said in the witness box to a question from Haight.

"We tested it off Port Lyness on the Welsh coast on our way to Liverpool."

"You feel satisfied that going 18 knots an hour - you realize that is 1800 feet per minute - that you could stop your vessel completely in only 2 minutes?" Haight asked.

"Yes, I do."

Haight looked down at his notes.

"Do I understand you correctly that you went up on your upper bridge and took the bearing of the *Storstad* range lights and estimated that the vessels were starboard to starboard before you could see the *Storstad*'s green light?"

"Yes."

"So you changed your course before you saw her green light, the starboard light?"

"Yes."

"When the fog came on, you never blew a running whistle of one long blast, which is the usual signal in fog?"

"No. I stopped my ship."

"So when you saw the *Storstad* lights become misty, you instantly stopped your ship?"

"I did."

"Is it usual when you consider that you are in a position of absolute safety to stop your ship entirely because the lights of another vessel look a little misty?"

"A fog bank was approaching from the land. I thought it my duty to stop my ship knowing that there was a ship in the vicinity."

"When you are absolutely in a safe position passing another ship green to green - left-hand passage - do you always stop your engines dead?"

"I considered I was in a position of safety, but I had no idea what the other vessel might do in the fog."

"There is no rule in fog which suggests running full speed astern or stopping dead?"

"I took the way off my ship, sir."

Galt stepped out of the Neptune hotel and ran into Ashby on the wooden sidewalk.

"Are you Mr James Galt, sir?"

Galt looked up at the insurance investigator.

"Yes. Can I help you?"

"The CPR sent me here. My name is Ashby. Can you spare me a few minutes of your time, Mr Galt?"

"Of course."

"I work for an insurance company in New York. I'm here to verify certain claims. You were a quartermaster on the *Empress*, were you not?"

"Yes, sir."

"Have they found the body of your colleague, Mr Sharples?"

"No, I don't think so," Galt replied.

"Do you know where he was last seen on the ship?"

"I think he was at his boat station, on the starboard side."

"Is there any reason to believe that he might have survived?" Ashby asked. "Could he swim or not?"

"I wouldn't know, sir, a lot of people were dragged down by the ship's rigging."

"Yes, I heard. It must have been awful."

"It was. Have you checked with the city, the police service?"

"Aren't they supposed to report the names of the confirmed dead to the CPR when they have them?"

"If they have found Sharples, it may take them a while to report it, what with the number of victims. I can take you over there if you like."

"Thank you, Mr Galt. I would appreciate it."

Ashby ran his finger down the page of the ledger on the desk of police inspector Mainguy. He was checking the names of some fifty individuals who had come to claim family members among the bodies on Pier 27. He stood up.

"Thank you, Inspector."

Mainguy closed the ledger and sat down.

"How are things going with the identification?" Galt asked. "I've heard the bodies are in a terrible state."

"It's going very slowly," Mainguy said. "It's not easy to identify a family member when the person has been in the river for a week. We're looking at watches, wedding bands, and pieces of jewellery. Sometimes a tattoo or a scar will do it."

"You don't happen to have my Mr Sharples among the victims, do you now?" Ashby asked.

"No, sir, but I would imagine that Sharples would be easy to identify from his uniform."

"Yes, I suppose he would."

"Sometimes people get lucky and the identification is quick. We had a woman in this morning from Peterborough who took no time at all to claim her husband's body."

Ashby pulled a list from his pocket.

"A woman from Peterborough? Could this be a Mrs Munro by any chance, Inspector?"

"Yes, how did you know?" Mainguy looked surprised.

"Her husband is insured with our company. Mrs Munro is doing the right thing, getting a death certificate is the first step in making a claim."

"How many claims are you expecting?" Galt asked.

"A good number on transatlantic runs," Ashby said, "life insurance is popular and relatively inexpensive. You know, it is quite common for a policyholder to simply disappear so the family gets the benefit. If the policy is for more than a thousand dollars, a woman can afford to shed a few tears and bury the man in her life, then in a month or two, she can marry the twin brother who just arrived from the old country."

"Yes, I see," Mainguy said, "so insurance fraud is quite common in your business."

"Yes, it is. In the trade, we call them the presumed dead, the ones that steal off into the night never to be counted. The smart ones never get found, the dumb ones stumble back into their former lives and then sometimes we get lucky."

Nineteen

"After you blew two short blasts to indicate you were stopped, what happened?" Aspinall asked Kendall in the witness box.

"On my starboard side, I saw the collier's masthead light and his green and red side lights bearing down on us."

"How far away was the *Storstad* at that moment?"

"About 100 feet away."

"How was he bearing from you?"

"At right angles to us. He was coming in fast."

Kendall remembered the horrific moment.

The Storstad's masthead lights washed over them coming out of the fog. Kendall watched the ship approach suspended in time before he jumped to the telegraph and ordered full speed ahead and hard-a-port to the quartermaster at the wheel. He then grabbed his megaphone and ran out onto the bridge, yelling to the other vessel.

"Go back, go back."

In the wheelhouse of the Storstad, Quartermaster Johannsen was at the helm with First Officer Toftenes and Third Officer Saxe standing by. Captain Andersen had just arrived and was checking the compass. He quickly ordered full speed astern and Saxe signalled the order to the engine-room, but it was too late.

The Storstad bow cut into the side of the Empress like a knife going through butter. Steel sliced through steel to a depth of 18 feet. As the men of the Storstad looked on in shock, a bronze plaque from the Empress cabin number 328 fell noisily onto the bow of their ship.

Kendall stood on the upper deck shouting into his megaphone.

"Keep your engines full speed ahead. Keep full speed ahead."

The Storstad bow slipped out of the Empress side and the ship swung parallel to the passenger liner before she disappeared astern in the fog.

"How long was the bow of the *Storstad* in the wound?" Haight asked during his cross-examination of the captain.

"It was a matter of moments," Kendall said, looking exhausted.

"A matter of moments, I suppose, would mean a matter of seconds?" Lord Mersey asked.

"Yes, a matter of seconds."

"How fast do you think the *Storstad* was going when she hit you?" asked Haight.

"10 knots."

"Now if the *Storstad* had a speed of 10 knots and carried 11,000 tons coal, it would seem very unlikely that she would come out of the *Empress* in only 3 or 4 seconds. Don't you think, captain?"

"It was the impact that drove her back. With the speed of her engines at that moment," Kendall said impatiently.

"You mean she struck you and bounced back?" Haight asked.

"Yes, she rebounded to a certain extent."

"Suppose for a moment, captain, that it was the *Storstad* that was stopped in the fog and it was the *Empress* which was moving along with a speed of 10 knots. Would not the result be the same?"

"No."

"Why not?"

"Not so rapidly."

"Do you think that the *Storstad* could swing you around with her engines going full speed astern faster than you could swing her around if your engines were going half speed or full speed ahead?"

"I do not know."

Aspinall exchanged a look with Superintendent Walters sitting next to Sir Thomas Shea in the crowded courtroom.

"I would like now to go back to before you entered the fog," Haight said. "When you first saw the *Storstad*, you had him on your starboard bow, didn't you?"

"Yes."

"So under the rules of navigation, you were required to keep out of his way and he was required to maintain course and speed?"

"Read the rule, please," Lord Mersey asked Haight.

Haight looked at his notes.

"Sir, rule 19 states: 'When two steam vessels are crossing, so as to involve risk of collision, the vessel which has the other on her starboard or right-hand side shall keep out of the way of the other.'"

"I don't quite follow the question," Lord Mersey said, looking confused. "If there was no danger of collision at this time, the rule does not apply. Does it or doesn't it?"

"As I understand it, my Lord, when vessels are on crossing courses, there is always the risk of collision, so the rule does apply," Haight said. "When a man sees a vessel off his starboard bow bound up the St. Lawrence and he is bound out into the Gulf, the rule applies and he must keep out of the way of the other vessel coming up the river."

"You consider that the *Empress* was crossing?" Lord Mersey asked.

"Yes, I do."

"I really don't see how this rule applies," Aspinall said.

Haight returned his attention to the captain.

"When you first saw the *Storstad*, you recognized that she was on your starboard bow?" Haight asked.

"Quite so."

"That then called upon you to keep out of her way and not to keep on your course?"

"The distance between the two ships was too great to consider any risk of collision."

"When you changed your course to north 76 degrees east and brought your vessel very much more towards the *Storstad*, did you not increase the risk of collision?"

"No. It did not increase the risk."

"Is it true to say that the change you made did bring you closer to the ship?" Lord Mersey said.

"Yes. It is."

"In your statements, you say you were stopped in the water at the moment of the collision?" Haight asked.

"Yes."

"You looked over the side at the water?"

"Yes."

"Did you not, Captain Kendall, make the following statement on the night of the disaster? You said to Captain Andersen: 'I wish I had gone faster.' "

"My Lord, I do not know whether it is wishful to tell this story," Aspinall interrupted.

"I wish to tell it," Kendall replied.

"Well, then, any objections, gentlemen?" Lord Mersey asked

the two lawyers. There was no reply from either man.

"Well, go ahead then, captain," Lord Mersey said.

"When I went on the deck of the *Storstad*, I ran into Andersen," Kendall said, remembering the scene.

Wet through and trembling, Kendall climbed aboard the Storstad and immediately confronted Captain Andersen in front of the Norwegian crew and the passengers from the Empress.

"Are you the captain of this ship?" Kendall asked Andersen angrily.

Andersen nodded.

"You sank my ship, and you were going full speed ahead in the fog."

"I was not going at full speed," Andersen replied quietly.

"You were going full speed, sir," Kendall insisted.

A Storstad man stepped between the two men.

"I wish I had gone faster," Kendall said. "If I had gone faster, you would never have hit me."

Kendall turned and headed for the warm interior of the ship.

Twenty

"Alice, I want to get off!"

They were in the playground in the park, and Alice was pushing Vicky on the swing.

"Alice, please stop," Vicky said nervously as the swing went higher and higher.

Alice was pushing hard on the swing and seemed distracted. She looked up at Vicky's frightened face and realized that the child was scared of the height. She slowed the chair, bringing it down.

"I'm so sorry, Vicky."

Vicky stepped off the swing and put her arms around Alice.

"Do you want to see the puppets now?" Alice asked her.

"Yes, please."

Alice and Vicky headed off towards the puppet show where a crowd of children was gathered.

"I think we've gone over it enough, Alfred."

"You think so?" First Officer Toftenes asked as he sat in a four-wheeled hansom cab next to Haight and Griffin on their way to court. The driver sat behind and above the men as he whipped the horse into a trot.

"Yes, I do," Haight replied. "Just stick to your story. Don't offer any information and don't elaborate. Stick to yes and no, and you'll be all right."

"This man Kendall, he does these crazy things. His story is a joke. How can they believe such a man?"

"He's a wily adversary, I'll give him that. He's a credible witness with the judges, but if you stick to your version of events, I'm sure you will get their attention."

"You think they will believe me?"

"I know they'll believe you."

"But they are British, Kendall is British. I am a foreigner, an officer on a small ship. You think they care?"

Haight looked at the young man with concern.

Alice sat in the parlour reading a letter. She looked up as Pauline came downstairs.

"A man from the CPR office delivered it this morning. Is it important news?" Pauline asked.

"It's from my sister. She's sending me a ticket for the train to Toronto."

"But you can't leave now."

"I'll write to her. Where's Vicky?"

"She's in her bedroom playing with her doll."

"I can't go home until this thing is resolved. I can't abandon Jamie."

"Don't worry, Alice. It won't be long before they resolve this misunderstanding."

"I hope so."

"Have you heard anything from Vicky's family?"

"No, nothing. I suppose the office will contact me when they hear from her kinfolk."

Captain Kendall woke up in the dim light of his room at the *Château Frontenac*. He was bleary-eyed and unshaven, with hair sticking out at all angles.

Johnson was sitting at the table playing solitaire.

"Whoa, you all right? You dozed off, bored to death by my company."

Kendall sat up.

"I have this terrible nightmare."

"I'd say that is not uncommon, old chap. See, most captains try to go down with their ships. When that fails, they've got to make do with the nightmares."

"I wouldn't mind a drink."

Johnson got up and poured them both a whisky.

"Now that's a good sign. Got your thirst back, have you? You can afford to, now that you've finished testifying. You did a good job, Henry. Walters looked proud."

"It isn't over yet."

"You think they'll call me?" Johnson asked.

"Absolutely."

"I better go in and have a talk with Walters. It might improve my memory."

Twenty-one

"You were the chief officer of the *Storstad*?" Haight asked.
"Yes, sir."
First Officer Toftenes was standing in the witness box in his cleaned and pressed uniform. He was a handsome young man, but there was a noticeable aura of sadness about his person. He had the disconcerting habit of looking his interlocutor straight in the eye with an earnest expression, which often left the person feeling uncomfortable.
"How long had you been aboard?"
"About three years and five months."
"What certificate have you?" Haight asked.
"Master's."
"You joined in what capacity?"
"Third officer."
"You subsequently were promoted to second officer and then chief officer?"
"Yes, sir."
"How long have you been going to sea?"
"Since 1895, sir, with the exception of about three years."
"Were you on the bridge at the time of the collision?"
"Yes."
"Was it your watch?"
"Yes, it was. From twelve to four."

"Who was on the bridge with you?"

"Third Officer Saxe and Quartermaster Johannsen."

"When you first saw the *Empress*, what was your course?"

"West by south magnetic."

"What light did you see first?"

"The two masthead lights and then the green side light off our port bow, our left side."

"So the *Empress* was showing her starboard light, and you were showing your port light. That would mean that she was on a course that would carry her across your bow?"

"Yes."

"Did you subsequently see other lights?"

"Yes, she changed course."

"How far away," Haight asked, "was the *Empress* when you first saw her green light?"

"She might have been three miles away," Toftenes said.

"Did you subsequently see any other coloured lights on the *Empress*?"

"Yes, after some time she changed her course and I saw her red light, her port light, on my port bow."

"When she changed course, what first happened?"

"Her range lights came into line, and then her red light came into sight."

"How far did she swing? Did the green light shut out or did the green continue to show?"

"No, her green lights shut out."

Toftenes remembered the strange behaviour of the *Empress* on that fateful night.

The Storstad, a dirty coal-laden vessel with a large white "K" painted on its smokestack, sailed into view, showing its red port side light. A bell rang in the wheelhouse to indicate an approaching vessel. Toftenes picked up the binoculars, standing next to the quartermaster at the helm and the third officer. He watched the huge passenger liner change course. Her range lights came together, and she showed both green and red lights until only her red light remained visible.

"How far was the *Empress* from you?" Haight asked.

"She was probably about two miles off, a mile and a half or two miles."

"What, in your opinion, was she doing?" Lord Mersey asked.

"She was changing course so as to clear us," Toftenes said.

"How did you suppose she was going to clear you?"

"She was, so far as I could see then, keeping on my port side, going clear on my port side."

"She intended, in your opinion, to pass you port to port?" Lord Mersey asked.

"Yes, my Lord."

"How long did you continue to see the red light of the Empress?" Haight asked.

"Two to three minutes."

"Then what happened?"

"The fog came in."

"Which steamer was enveloped in the fog first?"

"The *Empress*."

"When the fog shut out the *Empress*, did you hear any whistle from her?"

"Yes. One long blast."

"Are you sure of that?" Lord Mersey asked.

"Yes, I'm sure of it."

"The master of the *Empress* has stated that he never blew a signal of one whistle," Haight said. "Does that change your recollection of it?"

"No, sir."

Rain squalls were blowing in from the west when, early in the morning, Godefroy, Simo and Françoise set out for Rimouski in the wagon. Minutes into their journey, it started to rain. Godefroy and Françoise pulled oilskins around themselves on the front seat to ward off the downpour, while Simo, wrapped in a tarp, slept soundly on a straw mattress in the back.

The countryside was flat except for a few rocky outcroppings and hills along the St. Lawrence River. After a while, it stopped raining, and the sun lit up the river with large bands of light and shadow moving east.

They arrived in the town of Rimouski with its railway station and wooden sidewalks around noon. They drove to the CPR office in the centre. Godefroy climbed down from the wagon and attached the reins to the hitching post before waking their passenger.

"*Monsieur Simo, réveillez-vous*. Wake up."

"Wake up," Françoise said as she pulled on the man's sleeve. He opened his eyes and stumbled off the wagon in his dusty clothes with straw sticking to his hair.

"Look at him, *Père*. He can't go into the office looking like that," Françoise said.

Godefroy quickly patted Simo down, removing most of the dust from his clothes, before they entered the office. On the walls, there were railway schedules and pictures of exotic destinations like New York, San Francisco, London, and Paris. They approached a clerk with a green visor at the booking window.

"What can I do for you?" the clerk asked.

"We have a man here," Françoise gestured to Simo, "who was on your ship, the *Empress of Ireland*."

"All the survivors from the ship have been sent on to

Quebec City, miss."

"This is my father, sir. He is a fisherman," Françoise said, pointing to her dad. "He works for you collecting the dead bodies. Yesterday he found this man floating on the river."

The clerk frowned in disbelief and turned to his colleague sitting at a desk behind him.

"Fred, do you have the passenger list?"

Fred nodded.

"Name please?" Fred asked.

"His name is Simo Juvonen. Here, look at the paper."

Françoise handed the scrap of paper to the clerk, who passed it back to his colleague.

"What class? First, second or third?" Fred asked, looking bored.

Françoise looked stumped by this question. She glanced at Simo and her dad, who offered no help.

"I think maybe third class."

Fred examined the passenger list and then looked at his colleague, shaking his head.

"He's not listed, Joe. He can't be a passenger," Fred said.

"We found him floating on the river," Françoise insisted.

"Are you sure he isn't a member of the crew?" Joe asked.

"Not possible, sir. He doesn't speak a word of English or French."

Simo started to talk loudly in a foreign tongue, getting angrier by the minute. Godefroy and François watched the meltdown with astonishment. His face became flushed as he made the high-pitched sounds of a crazy man. He lunged at Joe in the booking window, grabbing his collar and pulling his face towards the glass screen.

"Hey, Fred. This guy's gone mad. Help me."

Fred stood up and came to the window where Simo was

spouting off some kind of gibberish and glaring at his colleague.

"Tell this idiot to take his hands off my buddy here."

"Fuckin' immigrant swine," Joe said.

"I'm calling the police," Fred said.

Godefroy quickly grabbed Simo from behind and removed his arm from Joe's collar. He pushed Simo away and straightened the man's shirt, nodding with respect. He turned to Simo and frog-marched him out of the office, followed by Françoise.

"*Excusez- nous, messieurs.* So sorry."

On the wooden steps outside the office, Simo collapsed, sobbing in a state of extreme exhaustion. Françoise went over to Simo and put her arm around him.

"*Quel merdier!* What's wrong with this guy?" Godefroy demanded.

"*Je n'en sais rien*," Françoise said, discouraged.

"Well, now that we're here," Godefroy said, looking at the hotel across the street. "Let's go have a talk with Bob."

Godefroy led Simo to the hotel, followed by Françoise.

RELATIVE POSITION OF SHIPS

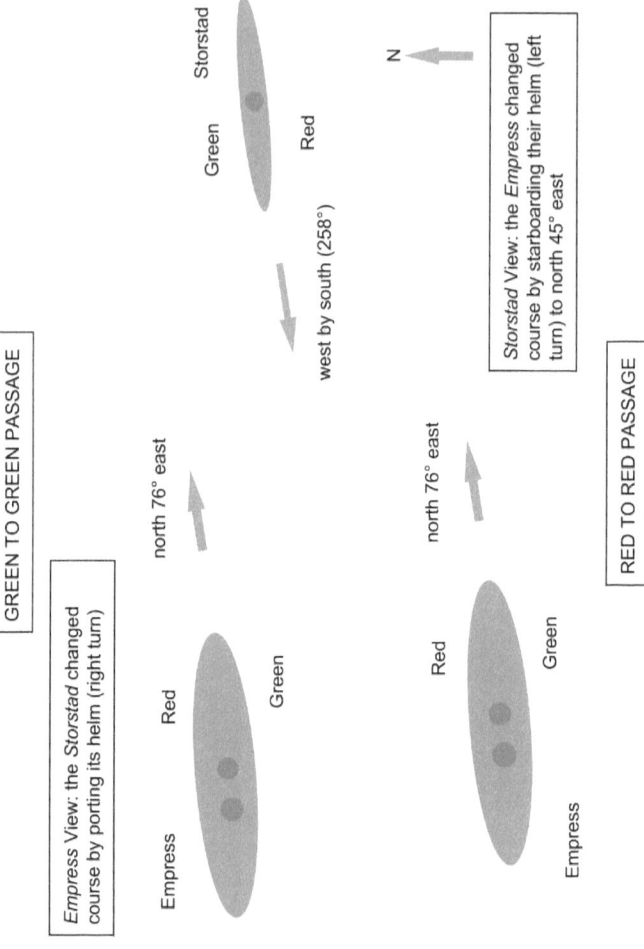

100

Twenty-two

At the hotel, Godefroy found Bob in his usual seat at the bar. He led Simo and Françoise to a table along the far wall and then joined Bob.

"Hey, Godefroy, old buddy. *Comment ça va?*" Bob said in a drunken slur.

"Bob, I'm gonna need your help."

"Let me buy you a drink. Whisky?"

"*Merci, mon ami*. My daughter is here with the survivor."

"The 'live' one?" Bob asked, grinning at Godefroy as he gestured to the barman.

"Yes, that's him."

Bob turned to look at Simo as the barman brought him a bottle and three glasses. Bob and Godefroy went over to the table and sat down.

"This is Françoise, my daughter. She speaks English better than me," Godefroy said.

"Well, ain't she a pretty young thing, Godefroy? You better keep a close eye on her."

Françoise looked down at the floor, trying to avoid Bob's leering gaze. She didn't like this drunken *anglais* from the city in his fancy suit and goatee.

"This is Simo," Godefroy said.

"Where'd you find this dago? He ain't French, is he?"
"No French, no English."
Bob poured the whisky and handed a glass to Godefroy. He poured another for Simo, who took the glass and emptied it in a flash.

"Damn, the son of a gun likes his whisky," Bob said, pouring another glass for Simo.

"I better let Françoise explain," Godefroy said.

Françoise frowned as she looked at Bob.

"My father found Simo floating in the river. We think he's a survivor from the *naufrage*, the wreck, you know."

"When did you find him?" Bob said, examining the girl with a lewd grin.

"A few days ago," Françoise replied.

"It was about sixty hours after the ship went down," Godefroy added.

"That's amazing. A live dago floating in the bloody river."

"He was hanging on to some debris," Françoise said.

"Still, he sounds like a fucking wagon-chaser. He probably found someone to put him out there. He's gonna want to make a claim as a victim of the wreck."

"He was very weak, sir," Françoise said. "He must have been out there for some time."

"You've checked the passenger lists?" Bob asked.

"Yes, we just came from there," Godefroy said.

"Well?"

"He's not on the list."

"What did I tell you, Godefroy? You should have left the son of a bitch out there on the damn river."

"We couldn't leave him, sir," Françoise said, shocked by Bob's words, "he would have died if we had left him."

"Well, you could always put him to work on the farm.

That's what I'd do, to pay what he owes you for saving his life."

Godefroy drank his whisky, looking discouraged, while Simo kept a close eye on Bob, hoping for another drink.

"You stated that you heard the *Empress* blow a long blast?"

Haight put the question to First Officer Toftenes in the witness box. Courtroom attendance was down after the busy morning session, but Walters and Shea were back, watching the proceedings with great interest.

"I did."

"When the fog enveloped the *Empress*, did you give an order?"

"I slowed my engines, slow speed."

"Did you blow any whistle after he blew his long blast?"

"Yes, I blew one long blast."

"Will you say what you mean by one long blast?" Lord Mersey interrupted. "What were you signalling?"

"One long blast is the proper signal for a vessel to sound when underway in fog, sir," Haight replied.

"I believe it is article 8 in the section headed 'Sound Signals in a Fog'," Judge Mcleod added.

Lord Mersey turned to Toftenes.

"You knew that?"

"Yes, sir," Toftenes replied.

"What was the next order you gave to your engines, if any?" Haight asked.

"Stop."

"When did you give that order?"

"One or two minutes after the 'slow' order."

"Why did you give that order?"

"Because I knew there was a ship in the vicinity and the fog was coming out from the shore."

"What was your speed when you were running 'slow'?"

"About five knots."

"So you ran slow for about two minutes?"

"Yes."

"What whistles did you hear from the *Empress* after you rang your telegraph to stop your engines?"

"Three short blasts."

"From the *Empress*' whistles, could you estimate the bearing of the ship? Were they on your starboard or port side?"

"I could tell they were on my port side."

'How many times did the Empress blow three short blasts?"

"I'm not sure how many times."

"You understood the meaning of the three short blasts?" Judge Routhier asked.

"Yes, sir. Her engines were going astern."

Twenty-three

A middle-aged American woman held a handkerchief to her nose as two men with scarves around their heads entered the brightly lit examining room in the temporary morgue on Pier 27. They tipped the body from the stretcher onto the table and hurriedly covered it up with a sheet as a constable approached.

"Madam Burke, please examine the body carefully. If you are sure of the identity, we will need you to sign the register."

"Yes, of course," she said as she took a moment to compose herself. "I'm ready."

Ashby appeared in the doorway.

"Am I too late?" Ashby asked the constable.

"No, sir. We're just confirming the identity."

Mrs Burke stepped up to the table and hesitantly turned down the sheet, revealing the upper torso of the young man. The tumefied face and body were in an advanced state of decomposition. Mrs Burke touched a mole on her son's arm with her fingernail as a tear rolled down her cheek.

"Yes, sir. This is my son Alan."

"Thank you, Mrs Burke," the constable replied. "Please come over here now and sign the register."

Mrs Burke sat down at the desk and dipped the nib of the pen into the inkwell before signing her name. She stood up quietly, a mother in mourning. Ashby chose this moment to approach her.

"Hello, Mrs Burke. I'm sorry to disturb you. I'm Ashby from the insurance company. I see you have found your son. Please accept my most sincere condolences."

"Thank you, sir."

"Do you intend to bury him here or take him home with you, madam?"

"I'm taking him home with me, Mr Ashby. The funeral home will prepare the body."

"Thank you, Mrs Burke. Good day to you."

Alice and Vicky arrived at the rooming house and were greeted by Pauline. Vicky rushed upstairs to her bedroom as Pauline pulled Alice into the parlour.

"*Il est arrivé*. He came around this afternoon while you were out."

"Does he know Vicky?"

"No, he's never met her. He's the uncle, the brother on the mother's side. His name is Donald Hayes. He's a farmer from Ontario."

"And his wife?"

"I don't think he's married."

"When is he coming to collect her?"

"Tomorrow morning, seven o'clock sharp."

"I'm going to miss her," Alice said.

"I think we both are," Pauline replied, putting her hand on Alice's shoulder.

Twenty-four

"How far away was the *Empress* when she altered her course?"

"I should say about three miles, sir."

First Officer Toftenes was under cross-examination by Aspinall.

"Then she altered her course, according to your story, and showed red on your port bow?"

"She did."

"Am I right in saying that up to this time, there had been no risk of collision?"

"There was not, in my mind."

"I only ask you this, in order to rid us of the Article 19 in the regulations that was mentioned by my colleague," Aspinall said as he turned to Lord Mersey on the bench. "May I remind your Lordship of the regulation: 'When two steam vessels are crossing, so as to involve risk of collision, the vessel which has the other on her starboard side shall keep out of the way of the other.'"

"This is what Mr Haight mentioned the other day when two steam vessels are crossing?" Lord Mersey said.

"Yes, sir," Aspinall said. "This gentleman agrees with me that there was no risk of collision up to the time that they got red to red."

"You thought the Empress was intending to pass you port to port?" Aspinall asked.

"I did."

"So, according to your story, the fog came on and you lost the *Empress* in the fog?"

"Yes."

"After she had entered the fog, you heard her blow one long blast. Are you sure you heard it?"

"I am."

"You are certain?"

"Absolutely."

"You were travelling at full speed when the *Empress* became enveloped in fog?"

"Yes. I rang my engines at slow when I heard a blow of one blast from the other ship."

"You lost her in the fog. You heard a long blast from her and then you rang your engines at slow?"

"I slowed before I heard her whistle as soon as I lost her lights."

"Is the last answer the right one?"

"The last answer is the right one."

"What whistle did you blow after you slowed your engines?"

"I blew one long blast."

"Then you heard the three short blasts from the *Empress*, meaning she was reversing her engines?"

"Yes, sir."

"You stated that you rang your telegraph to stop your vessel just before hearing the three short blasts from the *Empress*."

"Yes, sir."

"You mentioned to my colleague that the speed of the *Storstad*, when running slow, was five knots?"

"Yes, sir."

"Would not a laden ship, when you slow and then stop her engines, carry away at full speed for some time?"

"We would carry some speed. Yes. It takes a few minutes."

"After you rang your telegraph to stop, you gave an order to port the helm and then put it hard-a-port. This would take your head to starboard or off to your right?"

"It would."

"You were wishful that your head would go to starboard, to the right?"

"No."

"Then why did you do it?" Lord Mersey asked.

"Because the current was against us and we were stopped. I did not want the ship to swing to port, to the left, towards the *Empress*."

"You ordered the helm a-port and then put it very nearly - I think you said hard-a-port?" Aspinall asked.

"I did."

"Is it not a fact that in consequence of your helm being put to port and nearly hard-a-port, your head did go to starboard and that is how this collision occurred?"

"It did not."

"What was your course after you put your helm hard-a-port?"

"West by south magnetic, the same course."

"What was the object of putting your helm hard-a-port?"

"The object was to prevent the ship sheering to port because she had no way on her."

Judge Routhier signalled to Lord Mersey that he had a question.

"Yes, Judge Routhier. You have a question?"

"Yes, sir. Mr Toftenes, does the tide if it is on one bow or the other affect the steering of the ship?"

"It does."

"If you are going, say a knot and a half or two knots, and you have a current of a knot and a half or two knots on your right side, your starboard bow, what will the ship do?"

"Very likely swing to port, swing to the left side."

"When you had so reduced your speed that your vessel would not answer your helm, was there a way of foretelling which way your vessel might sheer?" Routhier asked.

"There was not."

"Would it depend on which way her head happened to stop?"

"It would."

Twenty-five

It was late at night when Toftenes, Johannsen, Saxe, and several *Storstad* men left a tavern to return to their ship. They were in an area of the lower town where the police patrolled in pairs and often in threes. It was a maze of narrow, cobbled lanes and alleys, overflowing with humanity and vice. There were gamblers, thieves, harlots, and drunken sailors on the corners, and the streets stank of vomit and spilled beer.

The *Storstad* men were about to exit an alley when a dozen Liverpool men stepped out in front of them.

"Bloody Norwegian swine," one of them snarled. "They ran our mates down, they did. Let's teach 'em a lesson, lads."

As the crowd of locals scattered, the Norwegians started to back up, only to find another group of drunken Liverpool sailors blocking their retreat.

Thor, a burly Norwegian with massive shoulders, grabbed a rain barrel sitting in the alley with one hand and stood with his comrades in the street. The Liverpool men surged forward, attacking the Norwegians. Thor swung the barrel like a sledge hammer and flattened two Liverpool men and then turned to face the attack from behind.

Toftenes was the first victim, struck on the head with a bottle. He collapsed on the pavement while Johannsen and Saxe tried to fight off their attackers. It was a losing battle until the others rallied around them. Thor laid out several of their assailants, single-handedly gaining the upper hand and driving back the drunken Liverpool men. This gave the Norwegians time to help Toftenes to his feet and move him out of danger. The Liverpool men soon had had enough as Thor led his shipmates out of the alley.

It was dark on the docks as the *Storstad* men helped Toftenes up the gangway. He was bleeding from a head wound, while the others had dirty clothes and bruised faces. They entered the mess room and sat Toftenes down at a table. In the light, he looked terrible with blood covering half his face and soaking his neck and clothes. Thor hurried into the galley and emerged a moment later with a towel, a bottle of schnapps and some glasses. He gave the towel to Toftenes and started to pour the schnapps as Frida appeared in her nightgown and robe.

"What happened to you, Alfred?"

"The Liverpool men were waiting for us," Toftenes said, as he applied the towel to his head and neck. "We were attacked."

Frida shook her head and went into the galley.

"Chimney sweeps, pickpockets, beggars, and the like," Thor said scornfully, "not good fighters."

"They hate us," Toftenes said. "Everyone hates us in this town."

"There were a lot of them," Saxe said. "Thor thrashed them nearly single-handed. Remember Danzig, Thor?"

"*Ja*," Thor grinned, "that was a real war. I broke my fingers fighting those big German dockworkers and their Polish friends. They were good fighters."

The cook, awakened by the commotion, appeared in the doorway as Frida returned with a washbasin and bandages. She sat down and started to sponge the blood from Toftenes' face and head, revealing the gash near his hairline. She looked up at the cook.

"Don't just stand there. Get me a needle and thread," she ordered the man.

The cook hurried away as she turned to Toftenes.

"I have to close it, Alfred."

"They will want revenge after what we did to them," Johannsen said.

"No worry. We'll knock 'em flat anytime," Thor said with pride.

"We better stay away from them," Toftenes said. "We don't want anyone to get arrested."

The men were interrupted by the arrival of a stranger in a rough coat and a flat cap who appeared in the doorway.

"Who are you?" Toftenes asked.

"I'm Evensen, Olaf Evensen. I'm here to collect my wife and child."

Frida put down the sponge and came over.

"Olaf, I'm Frida."

"I know who you are."

"Agnes and Niels are sleeping."

"Please wake Agnes so we can be off."

"It's late. She's sleeping. She's exhausted from her trip."

"I'm not leaving without my wife and child, Frida," Olaf said, standing his ground.

Toftenes stood up, holding the towel to his face.

"Mr Evensen, please come back tomorrow."

"You're the cousin, aren't you?" Olaf asked, recognizing the family traits. "What ever happened to you?"

"It's none of your business, Olaf," Toftenes said. "Please leave now."

Olaf stood his ground, unwilling to move until Thor came over to help.

"Alfred, didn't you just tell this man to leave?"

"Yes, I did."

Olaf got a good look at the giant Norwegian and decided that leaving was the better option. He turned on his heels and walked quickly out of the mess as the men laughed.

Twenty-six

"How you been keeping, Miss Vicky?"

A short, stocky sunburned man with enormous hands, sat in the parlour talking to Pauline as Vicky and Alice appeared in the hall of the rooming house.

Vicky shook Uncle Donald's outstretched hand but refused to look at him.

"I'm your uncle, Vicky. Your mama was my sister."

Vicky turned her back on the new arrival with a petulant air.

"You are being very rude, Vicky," Alice said. "Your uncle has come a long way to see you."

Donald looked bewildered and uneasy as he observed his niece's behaviour.

"She'll be all right," Pauline said. "Are you staying over?"

"No, ma'am, I ain't," Donald said, "I gotta get back to the farm. I went by the morgue down on the wharf this morning, but they have no trace of my sister and her husband."

"I'm sorry to hear that," Pauline replied.

Alice knelt near Vicky, embracing the child.

"It'll be fun on the farm, Vicky," Alice said. "You'll like it, I'm sure."

"Hey, Vicky, we gotta a lot of animals on the farm. Cows, chickens, a horse and even a goat."

"Time to go, dear," Pauline said.

With a scowl on her face, Vicky seized Uncle Donald's hand and pulled him towards the door.

"Well, thank you ladies," Donald said. "We really appreciate it, all the help you have given the child."

Vicky pulled her uncle over the threshold without looking back and started down the stairs to the consternation of the two women. There was no time to say goodbye.

"So the husband is returning today to collect his wife and child?"

Captain Andersen and Frida were having a late breakfast in the *Storstad* mess room.

"Yes, he is," replied Frida.

"Well, there is nothing you can do about it, Frida. She's his wife. Stay out of it, I say."

"I will not, Thomas. Agnes is my sister, she's family."

"You cannot prevent Olaf from taking his wife and child home. It's his right."

Frida glared at her husband.

"I don't care about his rights. He beats his wife. He has no rights."

Andersen suddenly realized that there was no way to win this argument.

"So what are you thinking?" he asked.

"You are the captain of the ship. You can prevent him from coming aboard."

"Me?"

"Yes, you. You're my husband. It's your duty to stand up for my sister."

"My duty? I have no such duty. Your sister is a married

woman."

"Yes, she is, but Olaf has lost any right to her. In my family, we do not condone wife-beating."

"She's married, Frida. The husband has a legal right."

"You will stand up for her, Thomas or I will leave with Agnes."

"You can't mean that Frida!"

"You heard me."

Agnes stepped into the mess room silently observing the angry faces.

"*God morgon*, Agnes," Frida said.

Captain Andersen nodded uneasily at Agnes and stood up, leaving the room.

"Tea, Agnes?" Frida asked.

"Please."

Frida poured the tea as Agnes sat down at the table.

"What was that all about?" Agnes asked.

"Olaf has arrived, my dear."

Agnes was suddenly alarmed.

"When?"

"He came by late last night and wanted to wake you, but we refused. He was very angry."

"I better get moving," Agnes said, standing up and looking around nervously.

"Sit down and drink your tea, Agnes," Frida said. "Don't worry. He won't be allowed back on the ship. I have asked Thomas to forbid him from coming on board. You're safe here."

"Are you sure?"

"Yes, Olaf won't be allowed to return."

Agnes sat down and drank her tea as she reflected on her situation.

"Thank you, Frida, but I need to go home."

"We'll book your passage on a boat to Liverpool and then on to Norway."

"What will *mamma* and the people in our village think when they see her daughter limping home from America with a child but no husband?"

"You'll be able to start again, Agnes. Nobody will beat you. It'll be a better life."

Agnes began to cry.

"You're strong, Agnes," Frida said, reaching out to comfort her. "You're my sister, we're a family."

"I'm not as strong as you, Frida."

Niels appeared in the doorway. He was wearing pyjamas and look at a water bowl near the door.

"Auntie Frida, do you have a cat?"

"Of course, we do, Niels. We have to catch the rats."

"Rats?" Niels asked.

"Big, ugly rats."

Niels looked wide-eyed at his auntie.

"Auntie Frida is exaggerating, Niels."

"I meant mice, my dear," Frida said. "The cats are here to catch the mice."

Twenty-seven

"I have had a chance to discuss your case with the coroner. Madam, your declaration concerning the birthmark of the child is not sufficient to prove he is yours."

"Not sufficient?"

Inspector Mainguy and Alice sat in his office with a load of *Empress* victim files on the desk.

"The coroner says that it does not prove that the child is yours."

"I don't believe this," Alice said.

"The coroner's position is that anybody could have noticed the birthmark and made a similar claim. You don't know how desperate people are to claim a body. Anybody is sometimes better than none."

"This is impossible, sir. I will not be allowed to bury my own son."

"You must find some proof, something more convincing. The Thompsons have provided a photograph of their child."

"I have no pictures," Alice said with frustration. "I told you before that I lost everything. I cannot believe that you have been taken in by the Thompsons."

"Please, madam, I do not make the rules. Find some evidence and bring it to me. It will then be my pleasure to defend your claim on the child."

SHIPWRECKED LIVES

Alice stood up quickly, turned and left the office in a huff. Mainguy sighed and sat back down. The job was starting to get to him. There were literally dozens of disputes between families claiming the bodies of loved ones.

"What were your instructions regarding fog?"
"To call the captain in case fog came in."
First Officer Toftenes looked exhausted sitting in the witness box as Aspinall questioned him. He had a few bruises on his face, but the hairline gash on his scalp was barely noticeable.
"And did you follow his instructions?"
"A few minutes after the fog came in, I called the captain."
"The St. Lawrence River is a river in which there is a good deal of fog and it is one of the great dangers of navigation. Is it not?"
"It is."
"I suppose there is a good reason why your master tells you that he wishes to be called when there is a fog?"
"It's a standing order."
"Why did you not obey this standing order and have him called at once?"
"I was not so particular about the time. I would sometimes wait a few minutes to see if the fog would clear."
"When the captain came up, did you tell him there was another ship?"
"No, I didn't have to. Almost immediately we saw the lights of the other ship on our port bow, on our left side."
Toftenes' thoughts returned to the moment in the fog when the lights from the *Empress'* bow had swept across the *Storstad* as the two ships closed on each other. Captain Andersen was

checking the heading of the ship on the compass when he shouted the order to put the engines full speed astern. Time seemed to stand still before Toftenes rang the engine-room telegraph with the new order.

Olaf Evensen arrived at the *Storstad* gangway and climbed to the deck. As he headed up the stairs leading to the mess room, a sailor on the foredeck popped his head up.

"Can I help you, sir?"

"I have come to fetch my wife and son."

"No visitors are allowed on board, sir."

"I'm the husband of Agnes."

"We've had several journalists sneak on board, looking for stories. Please, go back down."

"I'm not a journalist, sir, I've come to collect my wife and child."

Meanwhile, an engineer in dirty overalls with a menacing look approached Olaf from behind.

"Off you go now, sir. Goodbye."

Olaf looked at the engineer and angrily turned tail, heading back down to the dock.

Twenty-eight

"You were the master of the steamship *Storstad* at the time of the collision?"

"Yes, I was."

Captain Andersen stood nervously in the witness box, replying to questions from Haight. In the courtroom, Frida and Toftenes sat side by side, listening to the captain's testimony.

"How long have you been in command of the *Storstad*?"

"Nearly 3 years."

"What happened when you went onto the bridge?"

"I went to the compass. As a rule, I always do that to see where the ship is heading."

"How was she heading?"

"West by south, half south on the compass."

"What was the next thing you did?"

"I only had time to see the steamer coming at us out of the fog. It came up on our port side, our left side."

"What light was the *Empress* showing?" Haight asked.

"The green light."

"The instant you saw the *Empress*, what did you do?"

"I ordered full speed astern."

"How far away was the *Empress*?"

"I cannot say, but I would imagine it was a couple of ship

lengths."

"That would be about 800 feet."

"Yes, from 600 to 800 feet."

"Now captain, as near as you can estimate it, what would you say was the speed of the *Empress*?"

"I should say eight to ten miles an hour or something like that."

"What was your speed?"

"My ship was stopped. I looked at the water when I came out on the bridge and I thought my ship was stopped, but the speed might have been 1 or 2 miles an hour at that time."

"From what you've said," Lord Mersey interrupted. "I understand that the *Empress* moved sideways like a crab and then threw itself against the bow of the *Storstad* poking a hole in its side. Is this your understanding of it?"

"Yes. That is as near as I can say it," Andersen said. "The *Empress* crossed our bow. There was little way on the *Storstad*."

"When the vessels actually came together, captain, what was the force of the blow as you felt it on your bridge?" Haight asked.

"I hardly felt it at all."

"Did you lose your balance?"

"No, not in the slightest."

"Loaded as you were, captain, was there any sign of a rebound when your vessel touched the *Empress*?"

"There couldn't be."

"Had you being going 10 knots, top speed, with your full cargo of coal, and struck the *Empress* about midships, do you think it would be possible for you to have backed away at the instant of contact?"

"If my ship had been going full speed with the weight that was behind her," Andersen said, "I think she would have gone right through the *Empress* and cut her in two."

Alice returned to the rooming house, her eyes red from crying. She stepped into the hall.

"Alice," Pauline asked, alarmed. "What happened?"

"The inspector didn't believe a word I said. He thinks I saw Jamie's birthmark in the shed and then used it to identify him. This is terrible."

Pauline took a puff from her silver cigarette holder and stood silently for a moment reflecting on the situation.

"Well," she said, "I think it is time to take direct action."

"What do you mean?" Alice asked.

Pauline was about to answer when they heard music coming from upstairs.

"Oh, no!" Alice said. "Vicky forgot her music box."

She hurried up the stairs to fetch the music box and went into the bedroom.

"What in the world?" Alice exclaimed, happy and incredulous all at once.

Vicky was sitting on Alice's bed, the music box beside her. The little girl squealed with delight at the sight of Alice and rushed into her arms. Pauline entered the room and winked at Alice.

"Donald had second thoughts when Vicky tried to run away from him at the train station," Pauline said. "He came back and left her with us for safekeeping at least until his crops are in."

Twenty-nine

It was lunchtime in the *Storstad* mess room and there was a lot of noisy chatter as Niels chased the cat into the room. The cat was looking for food scraps. Niels crawled under the table looking for it, but when he stood up again, he spotted the teddy bear with the red ribbon sitting next to a bottle of aquavit.

"You like my teddy bear?" Thor asked Niels.

"Why's he got a red ribbon?"

"I don't know. Maybe it's for luck."

"Maybe he won it at a fair?" Niels said.

"Sure. Maybe he's a royal teddy bear, who knows."

"A royal teddy bear?" Niels asked.

"Sure, why not?" Thor said as he pushed the teddy bear closer to Niels's outstretched hands.

"Can I hold him?" Niels asked.

"Go ahead, boy."

"Where'd you find him?"

"Oh, it's a long story. We found him floating in the water the night the *Empress* went down. I think he belonged to a boy about your age."

Agnes entered the room with plates of food for Niels and herself. She put the plates on the table.

"Niels, come and eat," Agnes said.

"Did you find the boy?" Niels asked, returning the teddy.

"No, we looked for him everywhere."

"Niels," Agnes called. Niels joined his mother at the end of the table and picked up a fork.

"Why's he sitting on the table?" Niels asked Thor while the *Storstad* crew listened quietly to their conversation.

"Well, that's a very good question," Thor said. "First, we had to dry Teddy out. He was full of water because he'd been floating on the river for so long. When he was dry, we decided to keep him here in case a boy your age came in to claim him. We put him on the table so he could keep an eye on the door."

Niels looked at the door and then back at the teddy bear. He smiled at Thor as he ate his lunch.

"You were the second mate in order of rank on the *Empress*?"

"Yes, sir, I was."

First Officer Johnson was in the witness box under cross-examination by Haight.

"Did you see the navigation lights of the *Storstad*?"

"No, sir. I didn't see any coloured lights."

"Then you do not know for sure if safe passage was green to green, left-hand passage, or not?"

"I suppose I could have told by the two masthead lights that she was showing her green light."

"Could you have seen the green light if you had looked?" Lord Mersey interrupted.

"I could with the binoculars."

"You did not see it?" Lord Mersey asked.

"No, sir."

"At what distance was this?" Haight asked.

"About four miles."

"When you have a vessel three or four miles away from you, bearing two or three points on your starboard bow and you can still see her lights," Haight asked, "is it not a rather unusual manoeuvre to put your engines full speed astern?"

"No, sir," Johnson replied.

"What was the reason, then?"

"To take the way off the ship and navigate with caution."

"With your experience, can you recall any other occasion on which your engines have been put full speed astern when the vessel was 4 miles away, green to green on your starboard bow?"

"I have not been in that predicament before, sir."

"Do you remember any occasion in which the engines have been put full speed astern with a vessel four miles away, no matter how she bore?"

"No, sir, not before."

Johnson looked around the crowded courthouse and noticed the captain sitting in the back row of the audience near Walters. Kendall didn't seem to be paying attention to the testimony and looked lost in a world of his own.

Near the river, there was a very narrow street called *Sault-au-Matelot*, where local tradesmen did business with sailors from around the world. On the corner sat an unremarkable Chinese laundry.

James Galt walked up the street and entered the shop with its Chinese letters and drawing of a washtub in the window. He gave the Asian girl a chit. She disappeared for a moment and then returned with empty hands. Galt smiled, nodding to the girl and left the shop empty-handed.

The dishes had been cleared away and Godefroy and his family were gathered around a pot of tea on the kitchen table. Justine returned after looking in on Simo.

"Is he asleep?" Godefroy asked.

"Yes."

"We cannot keep him, Justine."

"I know, I know - but we cannot throw him out!" Justine said, wiping her hands on a dish towel.

"We must get him to Quebec City, *Père*," Françoise said. "He's got to be on the passenger list somewhere."

"Bob thinks he's a wagon-chaser, but I don't believe it," Godefroy said. "He would have died, had we left him out there for another day."

"I think he's crazy," Louis said. "I don't think he's normal."

"I say we put him on the train for Quebec," Thomas said.

"Let the Ursulines look after him," Marie said. "The church can pay his fare. It's not our responsibility."

"But who will pay for his room and board, and the doctor's visit?" Justine asked. "We're forgetting that he may be worth something. The CPR doesn't pay much for cadavers, but they might pay your father a lot more for a survivor."

"We have to take him to the city or we won't get paid," Françoise concluded.

Godefroy looked undecided.

"We could take him on the boat," Thomas said, "make a trip out of it and pick up the spare parts at the same time."

Thirty

"Why didn't you leave the other day?" Walters demanded. "Your passage was booked."

"My laundry, sir," Galt replied, standing in the doorway to Walter's office.

"What about your laundry?"

"My laundry wasn't ready, sir."

"So take the next ship, Galt. Peters will arrange your passage."

"Fine, thank you, sir."

Galt turned to leave but remained fixed in place.

"What else is on your mind, Galt?"

"I want to make a statement, sir."

Peters interrupted Walters as he came in with some papers to be signed.

"If you have a complaint to make, talk to the solicitors, Galt. I'm booking your passage on the next steamer, so don't miss it this time."

Walters signed the papers as Galt nodded and left.

In the ship's galley, Frida was preparing the evening meal with the cook. She was cutting green beans on a wooden board when Olaf Evensen and a stout Quebec policeman knocked on the door.

"Hello, madam. I'm Sergeant Walsh and this is Mr Olaf Evensen. He's looking for his wife and child."

"They're hiding them," Olaf said, glaring at Frida.

"Calm down, now. Let's see what they have to say. Is the captain here, madam?"

"Captain Andersen is not here, sir," Frida said, calmly wiping her hands on her apron.

"You are the sister, are you not?" the constable asked.

"Yes, sir."

"She's hiding Agnes, I know it," Olaf said.

"Is it true that you are hiding his wife and child, madam?"

"No, sir."

"Well, where are they, then?"

"Agnes left for New York on the midday train with her son."

The policeman turned to Olaf with a self-satisfied smirk.

"Well, it looks like you're a bit too late, sir. She's flown the coop as it were."

"I don't believe this woman," Olaf said. "We need to search the ship. Agnes was here only this morning."

"She left five minutes after you came on board, Olaf," Frida said. "You better get to New York real quick if you want to catch her."

"Look, Mr Evensen," the constable said. "The woman has spoken. Your wife is not here. That's good enough for me. Let's leave them to their cooking. I think you have a train to catch."

"I tell you the bitch is lying," Olaf complained as he left with the constable.

Frida removed her apron and went to the captain's cabin, knocking gently on the door. Agnes opened the door and embraced her sister.

"You're unbelievable, Frida. I heard everything."

"I hope he chases your train all the way to New York," Frida said, laughing.

"It gives us more time," Agnes said with a sigh.

"He can be in New York tomorrow and back again in 2-3 days. We need to book your passage for Liverpool."

Olaf hurried into the station to catch the train back to Montreal and then on to New York. As he waited in the queue at the ticket counter with his bag, he noticed a shipping agency next door with large posters announcing transatlantic voyages. He left the queue and entered the shipping agency.

Olaf approached the front desk, where a man was wiping down the counter with a rag.

"Good day, sir. Can I help you?" the clerk asked.

"I want to inquire about ships leaving New York for Europe."

"Yes, sir. When do you want to leave?"

"As soon as possible."

"There's nothing until Wednesday. The Holland America line to Rotterdam, the Red Star to Liverpool on Saturday, and the Norddeutscher Lloyd to Bremen on Monday. You could save yourself the train ticket and take the S/S Calgarian to Liverpool, leaving Quebec on Tuesday if you wish."

Olaf noted the multitude of passenger liners on the transatlantic run.

"Thank you. I need to get to Norway."

"Well, sir. The Liverpool ticket is the cheapest, then on to Hull by rail. That's a seven-hour trip by train and the ship to Kristiansand adds another 36 hours. In ten days you're home."

It was late in the evening as Galt walked casually down the hall from the lift in the *Château Frontenac*. He stopped at a door halfway down and knocked lightly.

A few moments later, Charles Haight opened the door in his dressing gown.

"Mr Haight, sir?"

"Yes. Can I help you?"

"I'm with the *Empress*, sir. They told me to come here to see you."

"Well, come in then."

Haight left the door open. A waiter appeared in the hall, carrying a tray, and knocked on a door to a room nearby.

Judge Routhier appeared in the doorway to collect the tray. He took the tray and tipped the waiter as Haight exited his room and crossed the hall.

"Judge Routhier, sir."

"Mr Haight, how are you?"

Routhier stood in the hall, holding the tray.

"I'm fine, sir. I think you should hear this. I have a man from the *Empress*, a witness. Can you come into my room immediately? This is very important."

Thirty-one

"Do you fancy a pirate story, ladies?" Johnson asked.

In a dark tavern, Kendall and Johnson were in mufti, having a drink with Murphy and two local tarts. The skinny one with the blonde hair and bad skin ran her fingers through Kendall's hair while the fat brunette with red cheeks sat back and pouted.

"I like pirate stories," said the skinny blonde.

"Henry, tell 'em your pirate story," Johnson said. "Nobody tells a better tale about pirates."

"You mean the pirate with the wooden leg, that one?" Kendall asked, slurring his words.

"Yes, it's a bloody marvellous tale," Johnson said.

"Well, ladies, this is the pirate story of all pirate stories," Kendall said. "A man was walkin' on the dock and spotted a pirate with a wooden leg, a hook, and an eye patch. He stopped the pirate and asked: 'You, sir, how did you end up with the peg-leg?'"

"A peg-leg?" the fat brunette asked as she leaned in, giving the captain a panoramic view of her large breasts.

"'Well,' says the pirate, 'we was in this storm at sea, a terrible storm and I was swept overboard into a school of sharks. And just as my men were pulling me out of the drink, a shark bit off me leg.'"

"Hey, come 'ere handsome. I like a man with blue eyes," the fat brunette said.

Kendall ignored the woman and pressed on.

"'So what about your hook?' asked the man. 'Well, while me and me chums was rapin' and plunderin' on the Barbary coast, I was caught stealin' from a merchant. I was arrested and they cut off me hand.'"

"Oh, that's awful," the skinny blonde said, turning to her friend. "Shut up, you old witch. He's mine."

An argument between two Liverpool men at the bar was getting progressively louder, so Kendall had to raise his voice to be heard.

"'Well, that's just terrible,' exclaimed the man, 'but how'd you get the eye patch?' The pirate just looked at the man and lifted his metal hook so he could see it, saying: 'A seagull dropping fell into my eye.'"

"'So you lost your eye to a seagull dropping,' the man said with a guffaw. 'Well,' says the pirate, 'it was only my first day workin' with the hook.'"

"Oh, no. Gotta watch them hooks," said the skinny blonde as the others burst into laughter. Behind them, the argument at the bar had escalated into a full-scale brawl.

"Hey, we better get outta here," the fat brunette said. "Come along."

The group struggled to get to the door. A chair was thrown and knocked the captain senseless to the floor as Johnson and Murphy waded into the fight. The two women grabbed Kendall, bleeding from a head wound, and staggered outside.

"You cannot come back here, sir," the technician in the white lab coat warned. Ashby was standing in the embalming room of a local funeral home.

"What's your name, young man?" Ashby blustered.

"Bigley, sir."

"Do you have Mr Munro's body in here, Mr Bigley?"

"Are you with the family, sir?"

"No, I'm not. I represent the insurance company."

Bigley stood his ground.

"Well, you can't be coming back here, sir."

Ashby noticed the body of a man on a far table. He reached into his pocket for a one-dollar Dominion bill and handed it to the man whose attitude changed instantly.

"Mrs Munro had a body sent over here yesterday. You wouldn't know anything about that, would you?"

"What do you need, sir?" Bigley asked.

"I'd just like to take a look at the body."

Bigley beckoned Ashby to follow him and they stepped over to the body in the corner.

"This is the husband?" Ashby asked.

The technician read from the file.

"Yes, sir. The name is William Munro. We are to prepare him for burial. The interment is tomorrow."

Ashby looked down at a rather stout individual with a beard and a lot of chest hair.

"How old would you put the victim?" Ashby asked.

"It says here that he's 44 years old. That looks about right."

"You see the scar - perhaps an appendectomy?"

"Yes, sir, it looks like it."

Ashby consulted a file in his briefcase.

"Do you think he is left or right-handed?"

"His left hand is large and more muscled," Bigley said. "I would say he's probably a lefty, sir."

"Good, I agree with your deduction," Ashby said, smiling.

"Let's get the measure of him."

Ashby handed Bigley the end of a tape measure and they proceeded to measure the body.

"66 inches."

"Noted."

Ashby wrote the height in a small notebook and said: "What about the weight?"

Bigley looked thoroughly annoyed by Ashby and the interruption of his work schedule.

"Let's put him on the scales," Ashby said.

The technician only complied with the man's request in the hope of earning another dollar bill. Grumbling, he pushed the gurney into the middle of the room where a sling was positioned with large straps to a spring weight scale.

Thirty-two

The room was awash with sunlight as Kendall ran water over his face in a room at the Neptune Hotel. Galt knocked at the door and entered the room with a towel, a straight razor, and a shaving kit.

"Thank you, Galt. So what the devil happened last night?"

Kendall fingered the cuts on his scalp before he lathered up and started to shave.

"Sir, you were bleeding badly when you came out of the tavern. You were in a sorry state."

"I was plastered, old chap," Kendall laughed. "I went arse over tit in that bar. Thank you for your help. You're a good man."

"You're welcome, sir."

Galt sat down and watched the captain shaving.

"I've been called, sir."

"Thinking of becoming a missionary, are we?"

"No, sir. The court, I'm to testify. A messenger just brought me an order to appear in court."

"Well, that is something."

"I've never been in a courtroom before."

"You'll do fine, Galt. Just be yourself. Look your man straight in the eyes and never hesitate."

"Is that the way, sir?"

SHIPWRECKED LIVES

Kendall nodded and started to shave.

The Thompsons were having tea in their richly furnished sitting room. Through the bay windows, one could see the neatly manicured gardens and the St. Lawrence River below in the distance. A maid entered the room and handed a letter to Mrs Thompson. She took out her glasses and began to read. Her features stiffened with irritation.

"What gall, what impudence that woman has! I can't believe it. She wants to take our little Robby away from us."

Her husband, a military man who was deaf in one ear from a bomb blast during the South African campaign, smiled at her as he worked on his stamp collection at the table.

"What did you say, dear?" Thompson asked.

"She wants to come 'round for a talk."

"What woman, dear?"

"That blasted woman who is trying to take poor Robby away from us."

"Oh, that woman."

"She wants to have a talk with us."

"Well, we could invite her for tea. Couldn't we, dear?"

"Over my dead body!" Mrs Thompson said.

Mr Thompson looked suitably humbled and returned his attention to his stamps.

Olaf had decided not to go to New York after all. Instead, he spent the morning watching the *Storstad* from a vantage point behind a shed on the dock. There was little chance of catching his wife and child boarding a ship in New York with its choice of transatlantic vessels. Money was another reason that he felt his wife would choose the more economical option of sailing to Liverpool from Quebec.

He was sure Frida had been lying about New York and was hiding them on the ship or in a cheap hotel in the old port. He just had to keep his eyes open and he would find them sooner or later.

He stood in the shadows and smoked a cigarette as he casually watched for movement on the upper deck. The crumpled bow on the collier was clearly visible. It had been bent out of shape during the collision and would require several months of repair work in a dry dock.

A grimy street kid in short pants and cap swept by on his bike, and Olaf stepped out of the shadows.

"Hey, kid. Wanna make some money?" Olaf yelled.

The kid stopped his bike and looked back at Olaf.

In the *Storstad* mess room, Agnes was sitting at the table as Niels played in the background with the teddy bear. The young kid from the dock stepped into the room.

"I'm lookin' for Agnes E-v-e-n-s-e-n?"

Agnes nodded at the boy.

"Are you Miss Agnes?" the boy asked again.

"Yes, I'm Agnes."

"I put the mail on the deck near the steps. There's a parcel addressed to you, madam."

The boy ran out as Agnes got up from the table and followed him outside. As Agnes went over to the railing, the boy was already running down the gangway. She watched him grab his bike and cycle away.

Olaf easily spotted Agnes on the upper deck and returned to his hiding place with a self-satisfied grin. It wouldn't be long before he caught up with her. She had led him on a wild goose chase across the continent at great cost during the critical seeding time on the farm. She was going to get her comeuppance soon enough. He would make her pay.

Agnes checked the stairs but could see no mail or parcels so she returned to the galley.

"Some kid is playing jokes on us, I think," Agnes said to Frida, who was peeling potatoes.

"Pardon me?"

"A boy just came in. He said that there was a parcel for me on the deck, but I couldn't find it."

"My husband collects the mail at the post office, Agnes," Frida said, looking alarmed. "They don't bring it to the ship."

"What is it?" Agnes asked, looking worried.

"Did you hide your face when you were on the deck?"

"No, I went out there looking for the mail."

Frida shrugged and dumped the potatoes in a pan.

"You think Olaf saw me?"

Frida nodded and said: "We must be very careful."

"But I thought you sent him on to New York."

"He might be in New York or he might not. He may be watching the ship."

Thirty-three

In the courtroom, James Galt sat nervously in the witness box, chewing gum as he waited for Haight to ask his questions. The courtroom was packed, and the judges were in a huddle discussing the appropriateness of the testimony from the new witness. After a moment, Lord Mersey nodded at Haight, who stood up and approached the witness.

"Mr Galt," he asked, "how long have you been acting as quartermaster?"

"Three and a half years, sir, for the Allan, White Star, CPR, and Harrison lines."

"Will you name a few of the steamers?"

"Virginian, Teutonic, Craftsman."

"How many voyages have you made on the *Empress*?"

"Two, sir."

"Have you finished your dinner, Mr Galt?" Lord Mersey asked, looking annoyed.

"Yes, sir," Galt said, confused by the question.

"The gum please," Haight said.

"Yes, sir. Sorry, sir," Galt hurriedly removed the gum from his mouth and got rid of it.

"Will you please repeat, as well as you can, the various statements that you made to me regarding the operation of the steering gear?"

"Mr Haight, that won't do," Lord Mersey interrupted. "You must not ask him to repeat what he said to you, but you may ask him to tell us of his own knowledge about the steering."

"Very well, my Lord. After you joined the *Empress of Ireland*, will you please tell us whether you had any trouble with the steering gear?"

"Yes, I did, going up the river in the place called the 'Traverse'," Galt said. "It is a narrow passage below Quebec."

"What happened?" Haight asked.

"I found it impossible to manage the vessel. When you gave her the helm, she wouldn't answer it in time."

"How much did she sheer off course on that occasion?"

"About three points."

"Was there any other vessel in the 'Traverse' at the time?"

"There was."

"Was your steamer sheering towards or away from her?"

"Sheering towards her, to port, sir."

"On which side was the schooner?"

"On our port side, the left side, sir.

"What did you try to do to correct the sheer?"

"The pilot gave an order to port the helm, sir, to turn to the right."

"Did you obey the order?"

"Yes, I put the wheel over to port about 15 degrees."

"Did it have an effect on the sheer?"

"Yes, for a time, sir."

Lord Mersey asked: "She went to starboard for a time?"

"Yes, but then she took a sheer back."

"So she took it into her head to change?"

"Yes, she would swing either way, from one side to the other."

"Am I to understand by this that she was turning to port

and to starboard?"

"Yes."

"At her own sweet will?" Lord Mersey asked.

"That's right, sir."

"By how much margin did you miss the schooner?"

"It was very close, about 40 feet, sir."

Superintendent Walters had been watching the proceedings with increasing concern. Now he stood up and made for the exit.

"My Jamie had a birthmark on his arm, sir," Alice said. "I told the inspector, but the coroner wants more."

A maid poured tea for Alice and Pauline, both of whom were dressed to the nines for their visit to the Thompson residence. Thompson received the women in a lounge suit with a white waistcoat and dotted necktie.

"I saw the child myself, Mrs Bingham," Thompson said. "The ruined face made identification very difficult."

"Then I don't understand, sir, how your wife managed to recognize the boy?" Alice asked.

"You know women. They can tell these things. My wife recognized Robby immediately. We sent his picture to the authorities."

"I lost my pictures of Jamie, but the child has Jamie's birthmark."

"I don't know what to say, Mrs Bingham. It's not me who will make the decision, but I rather think that nice police detective."

"He's my only child, Mr Thompson, he's my only child."

"Alice, I think we should be going," Pauline said, standing up suddenly. "We have taken up enough of your time. Thank you, Mr Thompson."

"Goodbye, sir," Alice murmured, heading for the door.

Thompson nodded and watched the women leave. He went to the bay window to look out at the garden where his wife was having a nap. How would this dispute end? His wife was dead set on claiming the body, but if she was mistaken, she would deprive another mother of burying her child.

Alice sat silently next to Pauline as the driver of the calèche took them through the park.

"We have not yet won the war," Pauline said, "but we've met the enemy. We'll find a way, Alice."

"But I have nothing new to show the inspector. I need some proof."

"We'll find something, my dear. It's not completely hopeless. There must be someone who saw the boy in Quebec or on the ship?"

"Well, there was a lady in the cabin next door, but I have no idea whether she survived or not. I don't even know her name."

"That's it, Alice, put on your thinking cap. We'll find something."

Thirty-four

"Were there other occasions when you had trouble with the steering gear of the *Empress*?"

Galt was in the witness box being questioned by Haight.

"On the night of the collision, sir. I was on duty from eight to twelve."

"That is going down the river?" Lord Mersey asked.

"Yes, going down the river," Galt said as he remembered the events of that night.

Galt had been at the wheel in the company of the Third Officer Moore and the pilot, a man named Bernier. Everything had been functioning normally until he tried to port the helm in response to an order from Bernier. The steering had jammed and Moore had hurried over to help. Together, they had struggled with the wheel, trying to free it by brute force. Bernier could do nothing but stay out of the way until the wheel finally responded and Galt gained control.

"How many minutes was the wheel jammed?" Haight asked.

"I cannot say for certain, about three minutes."

"During that time, were you able to steer the boat?"

"I was not, sir."

"Did you report it?"

"Yes, to Mr Moore."

"Is Mr Moore alive?" Lord Mersey asked the witness.
"He is not, sir."
"Did you report it to the pilot?"
"The pilot knew it, sir."
"The pilot is alive, is he?" Lord Mersey asked.
"Yes, sir."
"Do you remember the name of the pilot, Mr Galt?" Haight asked Galt.
"His name is Bernier."
"Was anybody else on the bridge beside the third officer and the pilot?"
"No, sir."
"Did you see the captain on the bridge at that particular time?" Haight asked.
"I did not, sir."
"Did Moore make any answer to you when you reported that your steering gear was out of order?"
"He said it would come all right soon enough. I told him if the steering gear was not altered, a collision was inevitable."
"What were you going to collide with?" Lord Mersey asked the witness.
"Nothing at the time, sir."
"Then there was nothing to collide with," Lord Mersey concluded.
"No, sir. But isn't the main asset of any ship the steering gear?" Galt asked.
"You are not going to ask me questions!" snapped Lord Mersey.
"No, sir."
"Did you have any other trouble with the steering gear on the *Empress*?" Haight asked.
"On my last trip down the Liverpool River."

"What happened then?"

"It was difficult to manage her."

"From your experience with other steamers on which you have acted as quartermaster, how does the steering gear of the *Empress* compare with the steering gears of other vessels?"

"It's altogether different. It's much harder to work the steering on the *Empress*."

"Where were you when the collision occurred?"

"I was on the forward deck, sir, having a smoke."

"Did you hear any signals blown by the *Empress*?"

"I did. I heard one long blast."

"So you heard one long blast, meaning the *Empress* was maintaining its course. How many times did you hear it?"

"I heard it twice. Then I heard three short blasts."

"Captain Kendall has stated that he never blew a signal of one whistle," Haight said. "Are you sure your recollection is clear?"

"I am almost certain, sir."

"What does that mean, that you are almost certain?" Lord Mersey interrupted, sounding deeply frustrated with the witness. "Who, in your opinion, is more likely to know the captain of the ship or you?"

"The captain of the ship, sir."

A horde of newspaper reporters suddenly rushed out of the courtroom to publish the Galt bombshell.

Thirty-five

The *Rose des Vents* sailed west with Godefroy at the tiller. It was a magnificent June day with bright sunshine and a good wind. Simo sat silently near the mast, watching the waves while down below in the galley Françoise prepared food for the men. At a sign from Godefroy, Thomas loosened the mainsail and the schooner tacked south.

Opposite the mouth of the Saguenay River, Godefroy pointed to a pod of beluga whales frolicking in the krill-rich feeding ground. The whales circled the boat, producing a cacophony of high-pitched whistles.

"*Françoise, viens voir,*" Godefroy yelled.

Françoise stuck her head out of the galley to look at the whales as they swam around the boat and smiled at her father. This was the first time that she had travelled with her father on the schooner and she was enjoying the trip.

"Listen to them whales," Godefroy said. "They don't call them sea canaries for nothing."

Ashby returned to the funeral home during the lunch hour. He entered the building, calling out to the staff, but there appeared to be no one around. He slipped into the embalming room where young Bigley was at work.

"Morning, Mr Bigley. How are you?" Ashby asked.

"Fine, sir."

"Have you seen Mrs Munro?"

"She left about an hour ago. What can I do for you, sir?" Bigley asked, hoping for another tip.

"Where did she go?"

"She went to the cemetery to reserve a spot for her husband. The body is being cremated today, sir."

"Pardon me?"

"She took it to the crematorium."

"I'm sorry, you said the crematorium?" Ashby asked, suddenly realizing the gravity of the situation.

"Yes, sir, the crematorium."

"Where is it?"

"It's not far. Take the road to *Anse-aux-Foulons*. You can smell it. It's on your right and has a large chimney."

Ashby ran out of the room.

Wolfe's Cove, or *Anse-aux-Foulons,* was a mile or two above the old town along the river. It was here that British forces commanded by James Wolfe landed in the 1759 battle for Quebec and had to scale the cliffs to engage the French under General Montcalm.

The crematorium was built in a rundown industrial sector known for its shipbuilding. There were empty dry docks and hangars along the shore surrounded by modest worker cottages. There was a lot of unemployment in the area due to the declining fortunes of the shipyards and the square timber trade.

A horse-drawn wagon was parked in front of the crematorium when Ashby jumped down from his hansom cab.

He rushed into the building and stopped in his tracks before the Dantesque image of a naked man being loaded head first into a coal-fired furnace on an iron sled. Two feet protruded from the door momentarily as the workers pushed the sled all the way in and then slammed the door.

"Stop. What are you doing?" Ashby yelled.

The workers in dusty caps and overalls immediately ceased work and looked at Ashby. One of the men stepped forward.

"*Monsieur, je peux vous aider?*"

"Get that man out of there."

The workers looked at Ashby as if he had lost his senses.

"You want to know the name, sir?"

"Who is it?" Ashby asked, as he realized it was already too late to save William Munro's body from the flames.

"The work order is on the wall, sir."

As the two workers looked at one another with sheepish grins, Ashby stepped over to the clipboard hanging from a nail and read the name. He heaved a sigh of relief.

"Where's Madam Munro?"

"The lady? She go to hotel," the first worker said.

"Where's the body she brought in?"

"*Suivez-moi, monsieur.*"

The man led Ashby to a row of steel tables where the bodies were arranged for cremation.

"This one," the man said, looking at the toe tag.

Ashby pulled the sheet off the face and recognized the man.

"That's him. Good, I'm going to need your help."

Ashby pulled a two-dollar Dominion bill from his pocket and slipped it into the man's hands.

"This is not the body of William Munro, you understand," Ashby said. "It must be returned to the port, so I am going to send a police wagon here to fetch it."

"There is a mistake?" the man asked.

"Yes, sir, there is. Do you have an urn?"

"*Bien sûr, monsieur,*" the man said with an air of complicity. "You want an urn with ashes?"

Ashby nodded, and the man stepped over to the wall and collected a dusty funeral urn from the shelf.

"Sure, that will do," Ashby said. "When Mrs Munro returns to fetch the urn, you give her this one and put ashes in it so it's heavy."

"Ashes, *monsieur*?"

"Yes, any old ashes will do."

The young man nodded, enjoying the subterfuge.

Thirty-six

James Galt knocked on Kendall's door at the Neptune Hotel. The captain, in suspenders, opened the door.

"How have you been, sir?" Galt asked.

"Fine, Galt."

Galt entered the room and hooked the captain's laundry bag over a chair in the sparsely furnished single room. There was a table and a dresser with a shaving kit on the bed.

"I picked up your laundry, sir."

"Thank you, Galt."

Kendall reached into his pocket and handed a twenty-five cent Dominion bill to him.

"Thank you, sir," Galt said. "Have you decided to move in here, sir?"

"It's quiet and almost empty now, with the men going home."

"I was in court, sir."

"So how did it go?"

"Not well, sir. I don't think they believed a thing I said."

"Well, don't let that get you down," Kendall said. "Did you look the man in the eyes as I told you?"

"Yes, sir, I did."

"Well, it can't have been so bad."

"I heard the whistle on the *Empress* that night, sir. The long blast. I heard it twice."

"Well, well."

"I cannot forget a thing like that, sir," Galt said. "I told them about the steering."

Kendall nodded.

"The steering mechanism was sheering badly."

"Well, you did your best, Galt. You told them what you knew. Nobody can ask you to do more than that."

Agnes, wearing a headscarf, climbed to the top deck of the *Storstad* and found Niels playing shuffleboard with a young sailor. The scoring triangles had been drawn in chalk on the deck.

"What are you doing out here, Niels?"

"Look *Mamma*. I put my disk in the number ten."

The sailor made a big effort to knock Niels' disk out of the ten but failed. He smiled at Agnes.

"Sorry Mrs Evensen, the boy looked bored, so I suggested a game."

Agnes nodded at the young man and walked over to the side of the ship. They were safely out of sight of the dock, but Agnes looked down anyway, in case Olaf was lurking there.

"OK, but keep him out of sight. We don't want his father to see him."

"Will do, madam."

Niels launched a new disk, slamming it into the sailor's disk in the eight.

"You see that, *mamma*?"

Agnes looked at her son and smiled. The fresh air and the game were doing the boy a world of good after their stressful escape from Minnesota.

"He did it, the bloody fool," Walters said as he dropped the newspaper on the desk in front of Peters at the CPR office. The headlines read: "EMPRESS STEERING GEAR DEFECTIVE".

"I planned to ship him out a week ago, but he wouldn't go. Shea will be out for blood now."

"He called already. He wants a meeting," Peters said.

"I bet he wants a meeting. Have you found Kendall?"

"We're looking, sir. He hasn't returned to his room."

"Find Johnson," Walters ordered. "He should know where the captain is."

The furious superintendent turned on his heel and went into his office, slamming the door.

The *Rose des Vents* was anchored near an island in the river at the end of a long day. Simo and the Paradis family were gathered around a campfire on the shore near the boat's dinghy.

The sun fell behind the horizon, painting the sky shades of red and pink. Silhouettes of birds flew off the water in the dusky pink light and gathered in the trees near Françoise, who was cooking fish over the fire.

Godefroy poured Simo a drink and one for himself from a bottle of whisky, as Thomas fed the flames with driftwood. In his usual manner, Simo emptied the glass in a flash, licking his lips. Françoise handed him a tin plate with a piece of fried fish and a crust of bread.

"Fish, Mr Simo, eat," she said.

Simo ate ravenously, stuffing the bread and fish into his mouth.

"His table manners are atrocious," Thomas said as he took

a plate from Françoise.

"He's probably just famished," Françoise said. "Don't give him any more to drink, *Père*. I think he's had enough."

"*Tu as raison, ma belle,*" Godefroy said. "He's a right, nice fella, but he drinks like a fish."

Thirty-seven

"You were quartermaster on the *Empress*?"

"Yes, sir."

Murphy was in the witness box being questioned by Aspinall.

"What time were you on duty?"

"Twelve to two, sir."

"Tell the court how the ship steered."

"The ship steered very good, as good as any ship I have ever been on."

"You have been quartermaster for how long?"

"Four years and five months."

"Were you on any ship before that?"

"Yes, the *Lake Champlain*."

"On the night of the disaster, you relieved your colleague James Galt at the wheel of the *Empress* at midnight. Did you not?"

"Yes, sir. I did."

"Did he say anything to you about the bad steering of the ship or that the wheel was not working properly?"

"Never, sir."

"Thank you, Mr Murphy."

Aspinall sat down as Haight stood up.

"I understand that you have never had any trouble with the steering gear?" Haight asked.

"Never, since I have been on the ship."

"And you found that it worked with absolute promptness whenever you put the wheel one way or the other?"

"No, sir. It might be that it does not catch and what you have to do is put the wheel back amidships and give it the helm and it will catch on right away."

"Sometimes when you put the wheel over, she does not catch on and then you have to bring her back amidships. Is that what you're saying?" Haight asked.

"That might occur every two years."

"It has occurred?"

"Only once since I have been on the ship."

"Your sometimes is rather infrequent then?"

"Sir?"

"Has she ever jammed with you?"

"No, sir, never."

"Well, when was the one occasion, Murphy?"

"Two or three years ago, sir, I am not quite sure."

Haight and Toftenes climbed down a metal stairway into the bowels of the collier *Alden*, a vessel similar to the *Storstad*. The ship was in port for some maintenance work. They arrived in the engine-room and found two men, up to their ears in grease, rebuilding a piston.

"This is Odin Sabje, Mr Haight. He's the second mate, he remembers."

Haight attempted to shake hands with Sabje, but hesitated when he saw the man withdraw his greasy hand.

"So you remember the night of the disaster, Mr Sabje?"

Haight asked. "The *Alden* passed the *Empress* coming up the river that night?"

Toftenes translated Haight's questions, but Sabje seemed to understand the gist of the conversation.

"Yes, we pass the *Empress*," Sabje said. "I can speak some English."

"Good. Are there any others who were on the bridge that night?"

"The pilot, sir."

"The pilot is a French Canadian, isn't he?"

"Yes, he's a good man."

"What time did you pass the *Empress*?"

"Around 9 p.m., sir."

"And she behaved erratically?"

"Yes, sir."

"Galt has opened a nest of vipers."

Sir Thomas Shea was pacing up and down the drawing room at the *Château Frontenac*, glaring at Aspinall and Walters.

"We don't have a leg to stand on," Shea said. "They have put in doubt the steering capacity of our ship."

"With all due respect, sir," Aspinall said, "I think we've circumscribed most of the damage with Murphy's testimony."

"I don't believe a word of it, Mr Aspinall. We haven't seen the end of it. It could be very damaging."

Shea turned to Walters.

"So what have you got to say for yourself, Walters?"

"I tried to send him home, sir."

"What about the others? Johnson, Kendall, the pilot?" Shea asked.

"The situation is under control, sir."

"I'll believe it when I see it. Haight has got us on the run, all due to the testimony of our own quartermaster."

"I don't think he made a very good impression," Aspinall said, "at least not with Lord Mersey, sir."

"Let's hope so. The judges may be on our side, but they will be swayed by public opinion. Gentlemen, you should see the telegrams that came in today. The insurers are nervous. The government is nervous. We are losing business across the board, ship and rail traffic is way down. So let's work on getting rid of the troublemakers, shall we, Walters?"

"Yes, sir. I'll personally see to it that they are shipped home."

"So what about bringing back Kendall?" Shea asked.

"It could help us," Aspinall said. "It all depends on how he performs on the stand. Haight has had him called already."

"The captain's disappeared, sir," Walters said, breaking the news. "We're looking for him."

"Disappeared? What the hell are you talking about?"

"He disappeared from his room and hasn't been seen for several days."

Shea looked at Walters, aghast.

"Well, you better find him fast. All we need now is for him to testify in favour of the Norwegians and we'll be out of business forever."

Thirty-eight

"You are the second mate of the steamship, *Alden*?"

"Yes, sir," Odin Sabje said from the witness box as Haight questioned him.

"On May 28, where was your vessel bound?"

"To Montreal."

"Did you pass the steamship *Empress of Ireland*?"

"Yes."

"Where did you pass her?"

"Six points off Cape Dogs near the town of Rivière-du-Loup."

"You were bound up the river and she was bound down?"

"Yes."

"At what hour did you pass the *Empress*?"

"Twenty minutes after ten, Sydney time, Nova Scotia time."

"Nine twenty Montreal time. Was the night clear?"

"Clear, yes."

"Can you get to the point?" Lord Mersey interrupted.

"I am just getting to it, my Lord," Haight said. "What was the first coloured light you saw?"

"Red, port side light, sir."

"From that time on, did you notice any problem with the steering of the *Empress*?"

"She was swinging, steering badly down the river. I saw the red light and then both lights and then I saw only the green one, the starboard light."
"And then what did you see?"
"I saw both and after that, red again."
"How many times did she change from red to green?"
"Between five and seven times."
"Did you make a change in your helm?"
"I gave a port helm, going to my right, about one and a half and two points."
"Did you fear a collision?"
"Yes, I was afraid. I was going to call the captain."
"Did you finally pass her red to red, a right-hand passage?"
"Yes, sir. I did."

Sitting with cap in hand, James Galt waited for Alice in Mrs Pelletier's parlour. Vicky appeared in the doorway.
"Have you come to see Alice?"
Galt nodded with a mischievous grin.
"Guess what I have in my bag?" he asked.
Vicky approached and stopped in front of Galt.
"Can I eat it? I like chocolate, you know."
"If you were a beaver, you could."
"Animal, vegetable or mineral?"
"Vegetable, I think. Beavers love it."
Vicky looked puzzled.
"I think people touch it for good luck," Galt added.
"Wood, it's made of wood, isn't it?" Vicky said excitedly. "Is it a game? I like games."
From his bag, Galt whipped out a beautifully carved wooden cup-and-ball. He held it up to a wide-eyed Vicky.

"What is it?" Vicky cried.

"It's a cup-and-ball game. You've got to catch the ball in the cup, like this."

He was showing her how to catch the ball when Alice descended the stairs.

"Alice, look what Mr Galt brought me."

"That's very nice, Vicky."

Galt removed a bouquet of red chrysanthemums from his bag and thrust them into Alice's hands.

"They're lovely, James," Alice exclaimed. "You shouldn't have. Thank you."

James smiled at Alice as Vicky tried to put the ball in the cup, but couldn't seem to master it.

"I saw your name in the paper, James," Alice said, sitting down near him. "You have become a famous man in Quebec."

"Infamous, you mean, Alice. I may never work on a ship again."

"You only told the truth at the inquiry. How can that hurt you?"

Galt nodded, looking resigned.

"I don't know anything about steering gears, but I do know you told the truth about the ship's whistle."

"You do?"

"Yes, my husband and I heard the single blast of the *Empress* as it entered the fog. It was what woke us up in time to get to the boat deck."

Toftenes was sitting on the bunk in his cabin on the *Storstad,* squinting down the barrel of a Luger 1906 handgun. He lowered the gun and began to load it with eight 9mm bullets. There was a knock at the door and he hurriedly put away the gun and the ammunition, along with a rag and a bottle of cleaning fluid sitting on the table. He opened the door.

"Alfred, I've brought you a cup of tea," Agnes said. "Frida sent me. She says you should get out more."

"Thank you, Agnes."

Toftenes took the cup and returned to his bunk, as Agnes remained in the doorway.

"How are you holding up with the inquiry?"

"It's OK. Our lawyer thinks we may be winning the case."

"Good."

There was a long silence. Toftenes had always been uncomfortable around women, and that was especially true with Frida's young and attractive sister.

"When do you leave for Norway?" he asked.

"Soon. We have tickets for the Wednesday sailing."

"Niels is a sweet boy. You must be very proud of him."

"He loves the ship," Agnes said. "I imagine he's a lot like you were at that age. You were always fascinated by ships if I remember correctly."

Thirty-nine

"My mother used to say that my dad was 'a boot with a hole in it'," Alice said. "'The more you pour in at the top, the more it runs out the bottom'."

Alice and James were walking along a path in the park overlooking the river. Vicky ran ahead as Alice stopped to look down at the river.

"One day, dad slipped and fell into a machine at the mill," Alice said. "He was drinking on the job, they said. He had a flask of whisky in his lunch box. They could only find bits and pieces of him. It was terrible. They put the remains in a cardboard box. That was all that was left of him, not enough to fill a coffin."

"I'm sorry to hear that, Alice. That must have been a terrible shock for you and your family."

Vicky returned briefly to show James that she had caught the ball in the cup.

"Well done Vicky, you're getting very good at it," Alice said as the child ran off again.

James took Alice's hand. She felt uncomfortable with the physical contact but was happy for the distraction.

"At my dad's funeral my mum cried, but we kids were relieved to see him gone. We were frightened of him because he was quick to anger and always drunk at home. You must think we were terrible children."

"You mustn't blame yourself, Alice. Children have no choice but to make do with the parents that sired them."

"After his death, a man from the mill came to the house and gave my mother some money that the men had collected for the family," Alice said. "My mother never remarried. I think she'd had enough of men for a lifetime."

They walked on.

"You must have seen my Tom playing with the Army band on the foredeck. They were to play at Albert Hall in London, you know."

"Yes, I'm sure I did. What a lovely sound!"

"So you saw them?" Alice asked.

"Yes, I did, and I also saw a winsome lass applauding from the gunwale with a hankie."

"You did not."

"Yes, I did."

Alice laughed, and James grinned at her sheepishly.

An elegant woman in her thirties, dressed in black and wearing a veil, waited in the dusty office of the *Anse-aux-Foulons* crematorium as a clerk brought her an urn.

"Here you go, madam."

"Thank you, sir."

The man put the urn on the counter.

"Goodness gracious," Mrs Munro exclaimed, "to think my little man is now nothing more than a pile of ashes. He wasn't much in life, but in death, he's a good deal less than I would have imagined."

She laughed, smiling at the humourless clerk. To satisfy her curiosity, she opened the urn briefly and peeked inside.

"Yes, I believe he's all there unless, of course, you're holding on to parts of him."

The clerk shook his head, shocked by the woman's dark sense of humour. He handed her a clipboard to sign.

"Good day, madam."

Clutching the urn, Mrs Munro nodded at the clerk and headed for the door.

"I think you will find it enlightening, sir."

Judge McLeod collected a file and handed it to Lord Mersey, who was sitting at the long table in judges' chambers. There were files and documents of all sorts, spread out among the litter of plates and empty tea cups.

"Of course," Lord Mersey said as he took the file.

A court clerk stuck his head into the room.

"Urgent telegram for Lord Mersey."

Lord Mersey stood up to receive the telegram.

"It's from the minister, Douglas Hazen," he said to his colleagues as he opened it.

"What does it say?" Routhier asked as he sipped his tea.

Lord Mersey's mood darkened as he read the telegram. He handed it to McLeod.

"PM DEEPLY TROUBLED," McLeod said.

"He's stating the obvious," Routhier said. "I'm hearing the same things in the press."

"The PM is worried about the political fallout from the inquiry," McLeod stated in a matter-of-fact tone.

"I won't stand for any interference, gentlemen," Lord Mersey said. "I don't think this merits a reply."

McLeod and Routhier nodded their agreement.

Forty

"How long have you been piloting the *Empress of Ireland*?"

"Seven years, sir."

The pilot of the *Empress*, Adelard Bernier, was in the box, being questioned by Aspinall.

"And you pilot her in the narrow waters, that exist between Quebec and Father Point?"

"Yes."

"Now in those narrow waters have you found her a good steering ship?"

"Well, sometimes we have to slow down to half speed."

"Would you call her a good steering ship?" Aspinall asked, impatient to get to the facts.

"Yes, of course. She was like other ships when they were given too much wheel and not easing in time, they would sheer."

"That is common with other ships?"

"Yes, certainly. It depends a lot on the man at the wheel. She wants to be watched closely."

"You know Quartermaster Galt who testified recently?"

"Yes, I do."

"Did he ever make a complaint to you about the steering of the ship or her wheel?"

"No, no complaint."

"No more questions, my Lord," Aspinall said, sitting down.

Haight stood up and approached the witness box.

"You stated, Mr Bernier, that sometimes you have to slow the *Empress* down. If you don't slow her down, what does she do?"

"In a narrow channel at 500 feet, I wouldn't dare to pass her at full speed."

"For fear, she might sheer into one shore or the other?"

"Yes, certainly."

"Now, if the man at the wheel does give her a little too much helm one way or the other, do you have to put the wheel hard over to counteract the sheer?"

"Yes, sometimes."

Lord Mersey interrupted the witness.

"The question is, did this man Galt complain to you about the steering gear?"

"No, my Lord. He did not and, if the thing did happen, I would have known it right away, because I always watch the tell-tale to see how the wheel is working."

"Did the second officer or anybody tell you that the steering gear had jammed?" Lord Mersey asked.

"No, sir. And she never jammed either, because if she had jammed for three minutes as Galt said, we would have known it."

Haight continued with his questions.

"Well, from the time the *Alden* was three miles distant up to the time you passed her, was your vessel going steadily on an even course?"

"Yes, she was steering fine at the time. I suppose she might have sheered a degree or two on each side."

"In your judgment, is it possible that she was sheering enough to shut out either light to a man in the position of the

Alden's bridge?"

"I was showing my green light to the *Alden*."

"Going for a left-hand passage. All the time?"

"Yes, until I was far enough down to port my helm to get clear. I didn't port or go for a right-hand passage before, because I was too close to the White Island reef."

"You passed on which side?"

"Port to port, red to red, right-hand passage."

"And how far off were you when you ported and crossed her course to show your red light?"

"She was half a mile ahead of me. I ported half a point, and we passed about a quarter of a mile of each other."

"If you were going 20 knots with the current and meeting a slower vessel going 5 knots against the current, it would take exactly one minute to run into the other vessel, if you were on a collision course, would it not Mr Bernier?"

"Yes, sir, but the conditions were clear."

"So instead of maintaining your course, you ported your helm and crossed to the right in front of the *Alden*. Why?"

"It was faster to get around her, by porting my helm, sir."

"Is it important to be a fast ship, Mr Bernier?"

"Of course. We have no time to waste, sir."

Forty-one

Mrs Munro was taking afternoon tea in the sunroom of the *Château Frontenac* when Ashby appeared in the doorway. He hurried over to her table.

"Hello, Mrs Munro. I'm Ashby, an insurance evaluator from New York. I work for several insurance companies in the city, including Metropolitan Life."

"Ah, Mr Ashby, I rang your company the other day about my husband's policy. My husband was William Munro. He drowned."

"Can you show me some identification, Mrs Munro?"

Mrs Munro pulled out a letter addressed to her husband from the insurance company and showed it to Ashby.

"Good, good. So you are the wife of Mr William Munro of Peterborough, Ontario?"

"Yes, I am. I came as soon as I could when I heard about the sinking."

"Have they found the body of your husband, madam?"

"Yes, I identified him several days ago in that shed on the docks."

"Good," Ashby said, taking some papers from his briefcase. "That means we can move forward with your claim."

"Would you like some tea, Mr Ashby?"

"I would love a cup, please."

Ashby glanced through his file on the husband as Mrs Munro poured the tea.

"So you identified the body, Mrs Munro. How did that go?"

"It was horrible, perfectly horrible: the decomposition, the state of the body."

"I understand. Here we go. Your husband was 5' 2" inches tall, 160 lbs. What was his profession?"

"Watchmaker, sir. He repairs watches and other things."

"How long were you married to him?"

"I believe it is now going on five years, sir."

Ashby nodded, looking at the file.

"Did your husband have any remarkable features? Scars, tattoos, birthmarks?"

"None that I can remember, sir."

"Was he left-handed or right-handed?"

"Right-handed," Munro replied after a slight hesitation.

Mrs Munro watched closely as Ashby made a note in the file. He took a sip of his tea and then looked at her.

"I would like to have a doctor examine the body as soon as possible. When is the interment?"

Mrs Munro suddenly looked concerned.

"He was cremated yesterday, sir. I have been here for a week already."

"That's very unfortunate, Mrs Munro, very unfortunate. We usually require an examination of the defunct."

Mrs Munro started to cry, pulling a handkerchief from a pocket.

"Please don't cry, Mrs Munro."

"It's been such a shock, sir, such a shock."

"I'll put in a good word for you, madam, when I talk to the company."

"Thank you, Mr Ashby."

"I have to go now. Here's my card."

Ashby handed her his card and finished his tea.

"When do you go home?" he asked.

"Tomorrow. I leave tomorrow on the train."

"Wonderful. Have a nice trip, Mrs Munro."

Ashby stood up and left Mrs Munro dabbing at her eyes with the handkerchief. She was confident that she had pulled it off. There was no way that Ashby could say the contrary. Her husband's ashes were resting in an urn.

The *Rose des Vents* sailed southwest past *Isle-aux-Grues* and the old quarantine station at *Grosse-Ile*, where the government mail tender was just pulling out of the harbour. The island was the main point of entry for immigrants coming to Canada and had been a quarantine station for the Port of Quebec since the 1830s. It had first been used to contain the cholera epidemic believed to be coming from Europe and later the cases of typhus among Irish immigrants in the middle of the century. Over 3,000 Irish immigrants were buried in the cemetery on the island during the Great Famine.

Godefroy sat at the tiller next to his daughter as Thomas and Simo were below decks having a nap in the cabin. Françoise was glad to feel the wind and sun on her face as she watched the islands on the horizon slip by.

"This will be your first time in the city, *ma chère*," Godefroy smiled at his daughter.

"I can't wait, *Père*," Françoise said eagerly. "I want to see everything I can."

"We won't be staying long, just the time it takes to get paid and to collect the engine parts."

"I know, but Quebec is a big city. There'll be a lot to see."

"Your mother has never been to Quebec. I have only been twice, and that was when I was a much younger man."

"I'm so happy to come with you, *Père*."

Godefroy in a rare display of affection, stroked his daughter's cheek and touched her hair.

Forty-two

"Captain Murray, what position do you occupy in the city?"

"I'm the harbour master, sir."

James Murray was an English sea captain in his fifties with a large moustache and penetrating eyes. He had sailed the oceans of the world and was a highly experienced mariner. He sat in the witness box, being questioned by Newcombe.

"Have you ever been captain of the *Empress of Ireland*?"

"I made three voyages on the ship this year, sir."

"You were also the captain of the sister ship, the *Empress of Britain*, weren't you?"

"Yes, sir. I took over command of the ship in 1906 and made 190 trips on the *Empress of Britain*."

"You had quite a successful run until two years ago when you ran your ship into the collier *Helvetia*. Is that so?"

"Yes, sir."

"When was that?"

"July 27, 1912."

"As I remember it, captain, you acted very bravely saving the crew of the *Helvetia* before it sank."

"Thank you, sir."

"But you were blamed for the collision, the reason being excessive speed, wasn't it?"

"Yes, sir."

"What were the circumstances of that collision, captain?"

"There was a fog in the river near Cape Madeleine east of Rimouski. We could hear the other ship, but couldn't see it, so I reduced my speed by putting the engines astern."

"How long were you running your engines astern before impact?"

"One minute and forty-five seconds, sir."

"What was your speed when you rammed the *Helvetia*?"

"At the inquiry, they said I was going half speed, about 14 knots before the collision. Judge Evans asked me what speed I thought the ship was going, and I said 3 knots. His Lordship thought that was a very short time in which to reduce the speed from 14 knots down to 3 knots."

Mr Haight stood up and approached the bench.

"Did you make an actual test to ascertain the time required to stop your ship when she was going full speed ahead?" Haight asked.

"Yes, we did the test near Liverpool when we were taking on our pilot."

"How long did it take?"

"Two minutes and 15 seconds, sir."

"You were trying to show by a practical demonstration that your statement to his Lordship was not an exaggeration?"

"Yes, sir."

"Now under normal circumstances, when there is no desire to show what is possible and your only object is to stop your engines and put them astern, the engineer does not throw his reversing gear and give her full steam astern in three or four seconds, does he?"

"I think he carries out the order given."

"Well, Captain Murray, how long have you been at sea?"

"Thirty-five years."

"You know, do you not, that there is no strain so severe upon a steamer's engines as to put them from full speed ahead to full speed astern without an interval of time between the orders?"

"Quite so."

"This is the most severe test that engines can possibly be subjected to?"

"Yes."

"At 18 knots or full speed ahead, how many revolutions is your engine turning over?"

"About 73 revolutions, sir."

"So unless your engines are exceedingly well made, it will wreck them, will it not?"

"No."

Lord Mersey interrupted the questioning.

"It is not a seamanlike thing to do, is it?"

"Well, it all depends on the occasion, my Lord. It may be necessary."

"Yes, I understand that, but unless there is some particular reason for doing it, some very imperative reason for doing it, you wouldn't do it?"

"No, sir."

When Superintendent Walters emerged from his office at the CPR, he was startled to find Galt waiting for him.

"Galt!" he exclaimed. "There you are. Have you seen the captain?"

"Yes, sir."

"Well, where is he? Out with it, man."

"He's at the Neptune, sir."

"What's he doing there? He has first-class accommodation at the *Château Frontenac* at company expense."

"I don't know, sir."

"The Neptune? I can't believe it."

Walters turned to Peters, who was listening to their conversation.

"Get me Kendall. He was supposed to be in court this morning. So what can I do for you, Galt?"

"It's about my return ticket, sir."

"Your return ticket?"

"Yes, sir."

"You bloody fool! You should have gone out on that earlier voyage and saved us all a lot of trouble. You cannot leave now. You're stuck here until the court dismisses you. Didn't Mr Haight explain that to you?"

"No, sir."

"You're stuck in Quebec until further notice."

"That's fine, sir," Galt said. "I just came by to tell you I'm staying over so I won't be needing a return ticket."

"Oh, so you've decided to stay."

"Yes, for the time being, sir. Thank you."

Walters nodded as Galt left the office.

Forty-three

It was Captain Andersen's birthday party. The tables in the *Storstad* mess room were laid with numerous plates and bottles of beer. In his Sunday best, Captain Andersen and Agnes danced to a Norwegian folk tune played by a member of the crew on a fiddle. Agnes looked striking with her pale skin and blonde hair set off perfectly against a black satin dress.

Niels was sitting in Frida's lap, watching as the men clapped their hands in approval. Nearby, Toftenes sat gloomily with John Griffin drinking beer in silence. Charles Haight came in, clutching his fedora to his chest.

The crew cheered his arrival.

"Sorry for being so late," Haight said.

"Just getting started, Charles," Griffin said.

"Whisky, beer, Mr Haight?" Toftenes asked.

"Beer please, Alfred."

Toftenes signalled for the cook to bring over some bottles.

"So what is the score, Mr Haight?" Toftenes asked.

"We still have a good edge over them."

"Not with Bernier's statement?" Griffin said.

"Damage control, John."

The cook arrived with the beer.

"'Damage control'. What does this mean?" Toftenes asked.

"They are trying to reduce our advantage," Griffin said.

"You Americans with your damage control," Toftenes said, shaking his head in disbelief. "Mr Haight, in Norway, a man is found guilty or innocent. There is none of this 'damage control.'"

"It's just a term we use, Alfred," Haight replied.

"You say this is America, Mr Haight. No, no. This is not America. This is Liverpool, this is Capetown, this is Hong Kong. This is what I think. This town belongs to the British. Here we are foreigners. They can do what they like."

Toftenes' words had a chilling effect at the table as Haight smiled, trying to maintain the good cheer of the assembly.

"Good evening, Mr Haight," Captain Andersen said as he came over with Frida to welcome the lawyer and his associate, John Griffin. Haight stood up to shake their hands and Frida invited him to dance.

"Tonight it is my husband's birthday party," she said, "but we are also celebrating my sister Agnes, who will be leaving us tomorrow."

"She's returning to Norway?" Haight asked as they moved around the floor.

"Yes, she's going home, Mr Haight. You are happy that things go so well?"

"Yes, thank you."

"But you do not look so happy."

"It's a complicated case, Mrs Andersen."

"So, you work hard."

"Yes, we work very hard."

"You must watch out for Alfred. He's never happy."

"Yes, I've noticed. We must try to keep up the morale of our troops."

"Yes, I think that is so. Alfred is my cousin. He's a very good sailor, the best, but he never laughs."

"Well, he provided excellent testimony in court," Haight said. "We were all very impressed by Alfred."

"He has the melancholy, you know, Mr Haight. It steals his heart."

"It's the curse, the Crippen curse," the Liverpool sailor said, slurring his words as he sat at the bar. The tavern in the old port was full of sailors and raucous laughter.

"What are you talking about?" his mate asked.

"Oh me God, you don't remember the dentist Crippen, who murdered his wife?"

"Crippen?"

"Inspector Dew from Scotland Yard arrested the man on the *Montrose*. Kendall was the skipper. It was in all the papers."

Dr Hawley Harvey Crippen was an American doctor who had been living in London in 1910 when he poisoned his famous wife, Cora Turner Crippin, also known by her stage name, 'Belle Elmore'. He had dismembered the body and hidden parts of it in the cellar of his house. He had incinerated the rest in the kitchen stove. The discovery of Belle's mutilated body parts launched a sensational crime story around the world. Newspapers immortalized Belle Elmore, the butchered star of music hall. Crippen was dubbed the 'North London Cellar Murderer'.

He fled to Antwerp with his mistress, where they booked passage on the first available steamer to Canada. The *Montrose* had barely gotten out to sea before Captain Kendall and his officers started to become suspicious of the couple.

"When they arrested Crippen," the sailor said, "he cursed the captain. He told Kendall he would suffer for his treachery."

"Cor blimey, the captain is cursed!"

The conversation in the tavern suddenly came to a halt as James Galt entered.

"Well, look at the devil hisself," the sailor said to his mate. "The dirty little scum who bites the hand that feeds him."

Galt approached the bar, but the Liverpool sailor stood in his way.

"Step aside, sailor," Galt said to the little man, blocking his way to the bar.

"We're Liverpool men 'ere, every one of us, and we won't have a scumbag like you amongst us."

A fistfight was about to break out, when an enormous beef of a man, a coal-stoker wearing a wool cap, stood between Galt and the sailors.

"I count five-to-one, Mr Galt. You don't stand a chance. Better leave well alone, my opinion, sir."

Galt nodded at the coal-stoker and retreated towards the door, as the Liverpool men yelled insults at him.

"Fuckin' traitor, scumbag."

At the door, Galt shook hands with the coal-stoker.

"I know you, don't I?" Galt whispered in the man's ear.

"Remember the night on the ship, sir?"

Galt looked at the man's face, but couldn't place him.

"You don't remember? You opened the hatch for the boiler room next to bulkhead five, which was breached. Water was flooding in. We barely escaped drownin'. You were with the third officer."

Galt recognized the man and remembered the incident. The men were so happy to escape the flooded boiler room; they had embraced officer Moore after closing the hatch.

"Moore is dead."

"Yes, I heard, sir. He was a good man."

Forty-four

Mrs Munro exited the lobby of the *Château Frontenac,* followed by a bellhop. A hansom cab approached, and the bellhop handed Munro's bag to the driver. She tipped the bellhop and climbed into the cab.

In the lobby, Ashby folded his newspaper and followed Mrs Munro outside. He glanced at the departing cab and then hailed his own. A cab pulled up and Ashby climbed inside, nodding to Inspector Mainguy sitting in the dark interior.

"So Inspector, any sign of our man?"

"No, maybe he'll be at the station," Mainguy said.

"Yes, he should be on the train."

They took the *rue des Ramparts* through the old city, following the Munro cab as it headed down to the train station in the lower town.

Inside the station, Mrs Munro hurried to catch the Montreal train. She went down the ramp and climbed into the nearest first-class carriage. From a distance, Mainguy and Ashby maintained surveillance on the woman, as a constable stood by awaiting instructions. They lost sight of her for a few moments and then caught a flicker of movement in one of the carriage windows. A porter was putting a bag in the overhead rack and Mrs Munro came into view as she sat down next to the window.

Ashby stood behind a newspaper kiosk, keeping well out of sight.

"We're looking for a watchmaker, a short guy with spectacles," he said to the inspector.

Several fat businessmen in frock coats and fedoras came down the ramp and stepped into the first-class compartment. A young woman ran down the ramp and got into the second-class carriage farther down. Finally, a short man with owl-like spectacles in a bowler hat headed down the ramp towards the train. He had a newspaper under his arm and climbed into the first-class carriage.

"Could that be our man, Mr Ashby?" Mainguy asked.

Ashby nodded and looked at his watch.

"Let's wait a few more minutes for him to get settled. We don't want to scare him away."

A train conductor came up the platform, looking at his pocket watch.

"Everybody on board for Montreal!"

Inspector Mainguy stepped close to the conductor and whispered in his ear. The conductor nodded and continued on down the platform.

"OK, let's go. He may try to do a runner, Inspector," Ashby said.

"Don't worry, we'll get him," Mainguy replied.

Mainguy nodded to the constable as they walked down to the train. Ashby followed the inspector, holding his hat over his face, as they climbed into the first-class carriage. Mainguy left the constable to watch the door, as they started their search for the watchmaker.

Ashby hid his face with his hat as he passed in front of Mrs Munro's compartment. Mrs Munro watched them go, but showed no interest. They moved on down the carriage and then stopped to consult.

"That's him," Ashby said to Mainguy, careful to keep his voice down. "He's in the second compartment back."

"Good, you stay here."

The inspector signalled the constable to remain in the doorway to prevent the man from escaping. He then stepped into the compartment and sat down opposite the target.

"Mr Munro?" Mainguy asked.

The man ignored him, looking around nervously.

"Mr William Munro?" Mainguy asked again.

Munro suddenly bolted for the door, and the inspector had to move quickly to stop him. He grabbed Munro by the arm, cuffing him as he shrieked his indignation. Ashby stepped into the compartment.

"Nice work, Inspector. Hello, Mr Munro. We've been looking for you."

"You're under arrest, Mr Munro, for body snatching and insurance fraud," Mainguy said.

"You're supposed to be dead, sir," Ashby said with a grin, "but I can see you are very much alive. Now let's go collect your wife."

Mainguy and the police officer hauled Munro down the corridor to Mrs Munro's compartment, only to find that the woman had vanished with her bag.

"She's gone, Inspector," Ashby said, looking into the compartment.

Mainguy yelled at his colleague at the end of the wagon.

"*Allez, la dame s'enfuit*. The woman's escaping."

The officer quickly stepped off the train and saw Mrs Munro swept up in a crowd of passengers disembarking from the neighbouring platform. He took off running.

Sitting under a parasol on the beach, Alice watched Vicky and James in their bathing suits playing in the shallow river water. It was a hot day in June and there was a large crowd of bathers in the water.

Vicky was paddling about in her rubber ring float and splashing James. He retaliated by putting his head underwater and imitating the spout of a whale, showering her with water. Vicky squealed with delight and struggled to get away from him. After a time, they tired of the game and headed back up the beach towards Alice, near a row of colourful changing rooms.

"How is the water, James?" Alice asked.

"It's lovely. Isn't it Vicky?"

Vicky smiled happily and reached for Alice's hand.

"Come on, Alice," she said, laughing.

Vicky pulled Alice in her bathing suit off the towel and they walked down to the water, hand in hand. Galt lay down on the towel, watching them.

Alice looked down at the shallow water with trepidation. She was standing ankle-deep in the river with her toes in the sand. Vicky tried to pull her further out into the river, but she refused to budge. She remembered her fight for survival floating on the cold river. There was no way she was going to bathe in the river that had taken the lives of her husband and her lovely boy.

Alice was torn by her desire to play with Vicky and her fear of the water. She turned to look at Galt, who held up his hands, miming a question. After a moment, she gave up and returned with Vicky.

"I can't, James. I can't go in. I'm not ready."

"Take your time, Alice. You don't have to prove anything to anyone. You go in when you're ready. I was thinking about lunch. Are you hungry, Vicky?"

"I'm starving."

"Well, let's see what Alice has brought for us."

He kneeled next to the wicker basket and removed several sandwiches wrapped in butcher paper.

Forty-five

"You are a regular licensed pilot on the river?
"Yes, sir."

The pilot Lapierre of the *Alden* was in the box being questioned by Haight. He was a small, compact man with the weathered face of an experienced mariner. He spoke English with a thick French-Canadian accent.

"On your voyage up the river on the *Alden*, did you pass the *Empress of Ireland* on the night of the collision?" Haight asked.

"Yes, sir."

"While you were coming up the river, she was going down?"

"Yes, sir."

"What light did you see first?"

"The port light, the red one on her left side."

"Then what did you do?"

"I showed her my red, and I turned about a quarter of a point and kept my vessel in that position."

"You were going red to red for right-hand passage?"

"Yes."

"Did you have to change course?"

"I had to alter it all the time. Porting all the time. She was coming at me and she was not changing course. She showed me her red a couple of times and then her green. I was afraid she would run into me, so I gave her more port. Then when she got within half a mile or three-quarters of a mile, she showed me her red light and we passed on the right."

"How much clear water was there between you when you passed?"

"She was about six hundred feet from me. It was nighttime."

"Thank you, Mr Lapierre. No more questions."

Haight sat down as Aspinall stood up.

"Do you know the pilot Bernier, who was on the *Empress of Ireland* on this occasion?"

"Yes, sir."

"Is he an honest, truthful man, as far as you know?"

"Yes, sir. He is a good, able man."

"And an honest man, a truthful man?"

"Yes, sir."

"When the *Empress* was doing these odd things, showing you first her green light and then her port bow, shutting it out and opening it up again, did you keep your full speed?"

"Yes."

"You were frightened of her?"

"We are all frightened when we see a big ship like the *Empress* with lights like an *arbre de Noël* coming before you and she is not answering your signal."

"You thought there was a risk of collision?"

"Yes, sir."

"'Is it not a good rule of seamanship when you think there is a risk of a collision to take your way off, slow down and possibly stop?"

"You sometimes have to wait to find out if there is a risk of collision. The *Empress* was a fast ship, going maybe 20 knots with the tide. We were very slow, you know, going against the tide, maybe 7 knots or less, so you see if we had stopped, we could not get out of her way."

Frida accompanied by Agnes and Niels, took a hansom cab around the *Bassin Louise* to the Louise Embankment wharf where the transatlantic passenger liners were docked. They were followed in the crowded street by an open, two-wheeled calèche with Olaf Evensen on board.
"Faster man, faster," he yelled at his driver.
The calèche soon caught up with the hansom cab, to the consternation of Frida and Agnes.
"Pull over, Agnes. I want to talk," Olaf yelled.
"Go faster, please," Frida yelled at her driver.
The driver whipped the horse, which took off at a steady trot, but the heavy cab was no match for the lightweight calèche. Olaf and his driver easily overtook the cab and cut it off. Olaf jumped out of the calèche, brandishing a gun, and ran towards the driver of the cab.
"Don't move or I'll shoot."
"Olaf. You can't stop us," Agnes said.
"You're coming with me. Come along Niels."
"He has no right," Frida said.
"She's my wife, and she's kidnapped my son. I have every right as the father."
Agnes and Niels descended reluctantly from the cab, while a small crowd of onlookers gathered to observe the quarrel. Frida watched Agnes and Niels climb into Olaf's calèche, and her heart sank. She boiled with indignation. This was not supposed to happen. Olaf had been waiting for just such a moment to spring his trap. She should have seen it coming.

The hansom driver handed their bags over to Olaf, who loaded them on board his calèche. Frida watched helplessly as Olaf's driver turned the calèche around and left. She looked up at her driver.

"I'm so sorry for the incident, sir. Please take me back to the ship."

The man angrily whipped the horse and they headed back to the *Storstad*.

Forty-six

Captain Kendall was back in the witness box under cross-examination by Haight. Walters watched from the back of the crowded courtroom.

"Captain, on your westbound voyage from Father Point up to Quebec, do you remember passing a two-masted schooner near the 'Traverse' below Quebec?"

"Yes, I do. We pass many ships on the river."

"Do you remember, in particular, your steamer taking a sheer in the neighbourhood of two points and passing very close to another vessel?"

"No."

"Have you ever known of an occasion when your steamer has steered badly to the extent of the wheel having to be put hard over to counteract an ordinary sheer?"

"No, never."

"Is it not possible that on the night of the collision when you were bound down the river and another ship was coming up the river, perhaps three hours before you reached Father Point, that your steamer sheered so that she first shut out the port light and showed the starboard, and then swung back and shut out the starboard, and showed the port?"

"No."

"Were you on the bridge continuously for the four or five

hours preceding your arrival at Father Point?"

"I was on the bridge practically all the time, except when I went below for a cup of coffee."

"Do you remember when you got your cup of coffee?"

"No, I do not."

"You have no recollection of passing the steamship *Alden*, a collier, between nine and ten o'clock on the night of the accident?"

"No, we pass many vessels at night. It's impossible to know their names."

"Did you receive any information from the officer on watch that your steering gear had stopped working?"

"No, none."

"Well, Mr Haight, you've got your answer," Lord Mersey said. "Can we move on, please?"

"One more question, sir. It is well known that the *Empress* ships hold the Atlantic record for the Liverpool to Canada passage. The advertising for CPR steamers proclaims: 'Fast service to Canada, only four days open sea'. So you must make good time on your way down the river?"

"Yes, we do."

"So when you passed the *Alden* on the night of the disaster and made the red-to-red passage at the last moment as described by your pilot Mr Bernier, with a quarter mile of safe water between the ships, it was to save precious time."

"My Lord, the captain doesn't remember the incident," Aspinall objected. "He cannot comment on it."

"I would like to reply to the question if I may," Kendall said. "The *Empress* was a fast ship, sir. So we did not need to wait for slower vessels to determine how we passed them. In the river, we had to avoid shallow water and hidden shoals, so we often had to change course to get around the slower ships."

"So if I understand you correctly, it is always the faster ship that determines the passage and it doesn't necessarily go according to the international convention."

"Safety is the primary concern, sir."

"I'm not sure I follow, Mr Haight," Lord Mersey said.

"The captain has just testified," Haight explained, "that fast ships determine the passage on the river whether it is green-to-green or red-to-red. The slower vessel has no say in the matter."

Haight picked up a piece of paper from his file and turned to Kendall.

"Just one more question, sir. I have heard that the fastest travel time for the mail from Moville in Northern Ireland to Father Point in Quebec is 5 days and 10 hours."

"I believe that was our best run, sir."

"Did you have this in mind on leaving Father Point, captain, to beat the record?"

"I'm not sure I understand, sir."

"With the speed of your ship, you could have avoided the fog and a collision with the *Storstad* by sticking with your original course from Father Point, north 50 degrees east, which would have taken you out into the river and towards the north shore."

"Yes, sir."

"But it would have delayed you, would it not?"

"Yes, sir, it would."

"Your course was into the Gulf and then southeast towards Newfoundland, was it not?"

"Yes, sir."

"Thank you, captain."

Frida was in an angry mood when she arrived back at the *Storstad*. Furious at Olaf and furious at herself. All she could think of was her sister being hauled back to a Minnesota farm for a life of beatings and servitude. She burst into the mess where the captain was having lunch.

"Frida, what's happened?" Andersen asked, looking at his wife with alarm.

"Olaf grabbed Agnes and Niels. The bastard had a gun and threatened to use it," Frida sobbed. "Agnes is my sister. I won't let him get away with it!"

"Well, I told you that Olaf had a right to his wife and child, but you wouldn't listen."

Frida ignored her husband and went to their cabin. The captain got up from his meal and followed his wife, still hoping to convince her to let it go. When he arrived in the doorway, she was throwing her clothes and toiletries into a cheap cardboard suitcase.

"I am going after them, Thomas," Frida said.

"Please, Frida, don't do that. You could wind up in jail for getting between a husband and his wife."

"I have made my case. There is no way I will allow my sister to be carried away like chattel by an abusive husband. I will kill the bastard if I have to."

Andersen looked alarmed by his wife's words and felt a desperate need to intervene.

"Let me help you, Frida. Where has Evensen taken her?"

"The train station. Where else can he go? He wants to put as many miles between himself and Quebec as quickly as possible."

"Well, that sounds reasonable. Which station, the CPR here in town or the Intercolonial GTR station on the south shore in Levis?"

"Why would he go to the GTR station?"

"The Grand Trunk railway will get Evensen and his family all the way to Chicago, and the seats are cheaper."

"I'll check the timetable for the trains," Frida said. "We may have a chance to catch them before they leave."

"I cannot leave the ship, Frida. John Griffin is coming by with some papers to sign within the hour. Take Thor and some of the men. Check the departure times at the stations. Be careful. You may still be able to stop Olaf, but don't confront him if he is armed."

Frida brightened with her husband's support and kissed him before running out of the cabin.

Forty-seven

Captain Kendall had gone down to the waterfront to get his mind off the stress in the courtroom. There were boats of all kinds tied to the dock: schooners, *goélettes*, coastal steamers, tenders, barges, ferries, shallow-draft lighters and harbour runabouts. He was strolling along the crowded wharf in a wide-brimmed fedora when he came across a ten-year-old boy scooping bilge water out of a wooden skiff. The boy looked up at him and grinned.

"*Monsieur, vous voulez aller sur l'île?* he asked. "You want to go to the island? I'm the *capitaine*, ten cents, sir."

"That sounds like a plan," Kendall smiled. "What's your name, lad?"

"*René, monsieur, à votre service.*"

Kendall climbed into the skiff as young René dashed about, mounting the sail. They pushed off and were soon on their way, sailing out of the *Bassin Louise* and crossing the bay to the island.

Kendall watched the lad skilfully sail the skiff towards the point of the *Ile d'Orléans*. He was wearing a flat cap much too big for him, but he didn't seem to care. A bright sun beat down on them and Kendall perspired in the heat.

"*Monsieur*, you know the *marée montante, marée descendante?*

I know them."

"I bet you know your tides, lad. The river current here is something fierce."

The boy nodded. René was not much older than his own son. Kendall's thoughts went back to his own youth, to the River Mersey on a summer day very much like this one.

Henry was in a sleek wooden boat with his parents and two sisters, sailing on the river in 1884. His father was a stern authority figure in his seaman's cap and moustache, quick to find fault and never a kind word. He had allowed Henry to take the helm and was now watching the boy like a hawk, hoping to catch him out, as he brought the boat around onto a new tack. Laughter was heard over the water as families gathered on the shore for picnic lunches.

"You're a very good sailor, Henry," his mother said.

"If he wasn't so serious all the time," his older sister remarked.

"I think he's doing a wonderful job. Don't poke fun at him, dear."

His younger sister was about to say something when Henry let the boat swing too much into the wind, losing its tack.

"Watch what you're doing, Henry," his father growled, grabbing the helm.

"It's not his fault," his mother said, defending him as always. "The girls were distracting him."

"Henry will never be a good sailor," he said, "if doesn't learn to pay attention. Now sit up and watch the sail, young man!"

Henry stiffened as he concentrated all his attention on the sail.

In the back of the skiff, Kendall realized that he had dozed off as the boy was saying something to him and pointing at the island. He looked over the gunwale and saw they had almost reached the island, which was dotted with summer cottages and beach fronts.

Forty-eight

Frida, Thor, and the *Storstad* men searched the CPR station in the city but found no sign of the Evensens. The next train was due to depart at six o'clock in the evening, so they took a ferry across the river to have a look at the GTR station in Levis. There was no sign of them on the platform, but since the train wasn't due in until three o'clock, Frida went to look in the waiting room.

She spotted the Evensens almost immediately. They were sitting among a large crowd of children on a school outing. She quickly backed out of the waiting room and hurried over to where Thor and his two companions stood on the platform.

"They're in there," she said. "I don't want to make a scene. Let me try to draw Niels away. There's a lavatory in the corner."

Frida went to a window that looked into the waiting room, directly across from where the Evensens were sitting. She put her face to the glass and made several hand gestures to young Niels, trying to get his attention without alerting his father. Finally, Niels looked up from playing with his teddy bear and spotted his aunt in the window. She put her finger to her lips, motioning for the boy to head towards the lavatory.

Niels glanced at his mother and Olaf, and then trotted off, heading to the men's room. Olaf was watching the school kids and didn't notice that Niels had left the bench.

Agnes became aware of her son's disappearance and spotted him standing near the entrance to the men's room. Olaf stood up and called out to the boy.

"Niels, come back here."

Niels ignored his father and stepped into the lavatory as Olaf took off after him. Agnes gasped when she saw Frida's smiling face in the window.

As Olaf entered the men's room, he ran into Thor and a *Storstad* man, chatting with Niels. He barely had time to look up before Thor slammed his fist into his jaw, sending him sprawling.

Frida ran into the waiting room and embraced her sister.

"Frida, what are you doing here?" Agnes asked.

"Agnes, come quickly."

"Where's Olaf and Niels?"

"I think Olaf may have had a little accident," Frida said. "Thor has Niels, we must hurry."

A *Storstad* man collected Agnes' bags, and they quickly exited the waiting room, joining Niels and Thor on the platform.

"Auntie, are we going to Liverpool?" Niels asked, hugging Frida.

"Yes, you're going on a long voyage with your *mamma*, young man," Frida said. "I want you to take very good care of her."

"I will, Auntie."

As they walked down the line of horse-drawn cabs to the Quebec ferry, Frida stopped Thor.

"What did you do with Olaf?" she asked.

"He was unconscious, so we left him sitting on the toilet, Frida. I didn't hit him very hard."

"Good work. When he wakes up, Agnes and Niels will be long gone. Thank you, Thor."

Thor nodded.

"Good, we better get back to Quebec. We're running late for the Liverpool boat."

They took the ferry across the river to the port of Quebec. When they arrived, Thor jumped off the ferry and ran up the ramp towards a stubby little water taxi that had just come in and was disembarking its passengers. Agnes, Niels, Frida and the *Storstad* men climbed onto the wharf and Thor waved them over. They quickly joined Thor and climbed into the harbour runabout.

"He'll take you to the ship," Thor said. "He says it's a ten-minute run."

"Good, we should make it in time," Frida said, looking at her watch.

Agnes and Niels waved to Thor and the *Storstad* men as the harbour runabout took off down the river with its unique putt-putt sound. The boat was about twenty feet long with oak planking, an interior cabin with windows all around, and an exterior sitting area. Agnes, Niels, and Frida sat outside with the wind in their faces.

A sailor came out to collect their fares.

"It's ten cents for adults, madam. Children ride free."

Frida handed over the paper money.

"Thank you."

Niels put his hand over the side to collect the water spray as the runabout headed towards the Louise Embankment wharf in the mouth of the St-Charles river. The *S/S Calgarian* was loading, moored in deep water.

The runabout dropped them at the ramp near the gangway leading to the passenger liner. The sailor carried Agnes' bags up the ramp to the wharf near a cluster of horse-drawn vehicles and motorcars bringing passengers to the liner. They walked down to the gangway of the huge ship.

"Have a good trip, Agnes," Frida said. "Forget about Olaf. I don't think he'll be bothering you again."

"Thanks for everything, Frida. Niels, give your auntie a kiss and a hug."

Frida embraced them both.

"Remember, you are strong, Agnes. Your family is with you. You can start your life again."

"Love you, Frida. Bye, bye now. I'll write."

Frida couldn't hold back her tears as she watched her sister and nephew climb the gangway to the ship.

Forty-nine

Captain Kendall was climbing out of the skiff with the help of young René when Galt spotted him on the dock. The captain paid the lad for the excursion.

"Captain, is that you, sir?"

"Hello, Galt. I have just been for a sail to the island with young René here. It's a pretty place on a day like today. How are you?"

"I'm fine."

René took off, doffing his hat to the captain.

"The boy reminds me of my son. I received a letter from my wife the other day. She told me that Tim had to read a poem at school and he chose Kipling: '*If you can keep your head when all about you are losing theirs and blaming it on you.*' You must know it."

"Of course, sir. It's a famous poem."

"A fitting poem for his dad, don't you think?" Kendall asked wistfully. "A man who lost his ship and a thousand lives."

"I doubt you'll be getting a gold watch for your service to the company, sir," Galt said, smiling. "They'll probably want to sneak you out the back door with the servants and the riffraff, so you don't steal the silverware."

"I dare say you're right, Galt," Kendall laughed. "I've put

the company to shame."

"You know Captain Smith of the Titanic. He lost his ship too."

"Yes, he did, didn't he?"

"He lost many more lives than you did and they had two and a half hours to save them - you only had 14 minutes, sir."

"With two and a half hours, we would have saved every last one of them."

"No doubt about it, sir."

"Thank you, James, for the thought. Please call me Henry. We're no longer on the ship, we no longer have a ship."

"Yes, sir."

"So what are your plans, James?"

"I will look for work, sir, but I doubt I'll find any."

"You think after your testimony that the Canadian Pacific will put out the word. I may be able to help you. Can I buy you a drink, James?"

"Of course, sir."

The *Rose des Vents* was dwarfed by the large ocean-going steamships already docked in the port of Quebec. Godefroy carefully motored the schooner into a small berth alongside a number of wooden *goélettes* used to carry cargo up and down the St. Lawrence. Simo looked listlessly around the harbour and made no move to help when Thomas jumped to the dock to tie the boat up.

As Godefroy busied himself, shutting down the engine, and Thomas attached the mooring lines, Françoise hauled a bag of rubbish out of the galley. She looked up at the dock.

"*Père*, where is Simo?" Françoise asked.

Godefroy looked around, but Simo had disappeared.

"*Merde*," he swore. "He was here just a minute ago. Thomas, go have a look?"

Thomas dropped the mooring line and ran along the dock in one direction and then the other. There were crowds of people about, including sailors, longshoremen, deckhands, working girls, and merchants of all kinds, hawking their wares. It was hard, if not impossible, to spot Simo among them. After a few minutes, Thomas gave up and returned to the boat. He looked down at his father, who was fiddling with the engine.

"He's gone, *Père*. We lost him."

Fifty

"What was the first coloured light you saw on the *Empress*?"

"I saw the two masthead lights and then the green light on the starboard side."

Third Officer Jacob Saxe of the *Storstad* was in the witness box being questioned by Haight.

"What happened next?" Lord Mersey asked.

"Then I saw both the green and the red light. The green then disappeared, and I saw only the red one about a point or two points on the port bow."

"You were then showing red to red and going for a right-hand passage?" Haight asked.

"Yes, sir."

"How long did the two vessels continue to approach, showing red to red?"

"A couple of minutes, sir, before the fog came in."

"Did you hear anything when the fog shut out the *Empress*?"

"I heard a long blast."

"So the *Empress* was telling you that it was staying its course?"

"Yes, sir."

"After the *Empress* blew one long blast, did the *Storstad* blow a whistle?"

"Yes, sir. One long blast."

"So after the long blast, you ordered your engine-room to slow."

"Yes."

"What whistle was blown on the *Storstad* after you heard the *Empress* blow the first signal of 3 short blasts?"

"One long blast, sir."

"I know several White Star captains. I could put in a word if you like. You could ship on the *SS Ionic* or maybe the *SS Athenic*."

Kendall and Galt were playing chess in a tavern near the docks. Galt moved his bishop.

"That would be much appreciated, sir," Galt said. "Careful now, your king is in danger."

"You're quite the chess player, James," Kendall said, putting down his glass of whisky. His attention returned to the game, and he moved his king out of harm's way.

"You know that the *Ionic* sails to Cape Town and New Zealand. It's a long way from the North Atlantic."

"Yes, sir. I see that, but I am not sure my mum and dad would want me to travel so far from home."

"I spent two years in Northern Australia on a clipper in the Timor Sea when I was your age."

"I'm not the adventurous kind, I think. My parents are elderly. They like to see me every couple of weeks."

"Yes, I understand. It might not be the best choice then."

"Checkmate," said Galt, taking a drink of ale.

"Very good. Shall we have another game?"

"Of course, sir."

Galt put the chess pieces back on the board.

"I heard you were a witness to a murder out there, sir?"

"Yes, I was. I was on the *Iolanthe* for five months in the Timor Sea, north of Australia. We were headed for Normanton in the Gulf of Carpentaria. We were carrying a load of steel rails for the new railway they were building in the outback. The morale was low and there was constant fighting among the crew. I happened to witness an American sailor kill a West Indian with a knife. I wasn't the only witness. It was murder, no doubt about it. The captain decided to turn the case over to the authorities once we arrived in port. Before we could get there, the other witness had been poisoned and died suddenly. So I became the target of the American."

"What happened once you arrived in port?"

"I had to testify against the man in an Australian court. I thought that would be the end of it, but the authorities threw out the case and sent the American back to the ship."

"You must have been worried for your life?"

"Yes, I was. I was just a young fellow, and this man was twenty years older than me. He was a bully and bore a grudge. My chances of surviving another voyage in his company were not good, so I deserted the ship."

"You deserted the ship?"

"Yes, I did. I ran away. I wanted to live."

Galt laughed.

"It's not very often that a captain admits to deserting his ship, sir."

"No, it isn't. But every captain my age was a young man once. I felt I didn't have a choice. I had to get away."

"Didn't your mates try to protect you?"

"Protect me? There was no way to protect me from a man with a knife in the close quarters of the ship."

"How did you get home?"

"I managed to stow away on a ship, which took me to Thursday Island in the Torres Strait between Australia and New Guinea. I worked on pearl fishing boats for several months before I was able to catch a ship returning to England."

"Your story is quite amazing. I wouldn't have had the courage to do what you did. It's your turn, sir."

The captain moved his bishop.

"Do you think I did a bad thing testifying against the CPR in court, sir?"

"No, you did the right thing, James. You told them what you saw, what you heard. You told the truth."

The captain took a pawn with his bishop, directly threatening Galt's queen. He sighed as he thought about how easy it had been in those carefree days to run off and abandon his responsibilities when no one was counting on him. After twenty-five years at sea and six as a captain of his own ship, he could no longer escape those responsibilities and had to stand with the owners.

Fifty-one

On a street in the old port, James Galt recognized the pretty teenage girl from Rimouski in the company of two rough-looking men.

"*Bonjour, mademoiselle.* I think we've met before."

"Hello, James. You remember me from the mass on the river? I'm Françoise."

"Yes, I remember. It was very moving to see the wild flowers floating on the waves. What are you doing here in the city?"

"This is my father and my brother," Françoise said.

"*Bonjour, monsieur Galt.* I'm Godefroy Paradis. This is my son Thomas."

"James Galt, sir."

"We're looking for a man, a survivor of the shipwreck," Françoise said. "We found him floating on the river."

"A survivor of the *Empress*?" Galt asked.

"Yes, my father and brother were hired to search for the bodies of the victims and they found a man alive on the water. He was in very bad shape, unconscious and dehydrated, you know. We had a doctor look at him and then brought him with us to Quebec in our boat, but he jumped to the dock and disappeared."

"Where could he have gone?"

"We don't know. He doesn't speak any English or French."

"He's a foreigner then, not from here?"

"Yes. His name is Simo Juvonen."

"I think that's a Scandinavian name. Where are you staying?"

Françoise looked at Godefroy.

"We're on our boat, James, in the harbour."

"Of course."

Third Officer Jacob Saxe of the *Storstad* was back in the witness box. As Haight and Aspinall looked at their notes, Lord Mersey put the first question to the officer.

"So Mr Saxe, when you were stopped for a few minutes, who gave the order to port your helm?"

"The mate gave the order to do it, sir."

"But why did he order it to be ported, turning your ship to the right?"

"I suppose it was to adjust the course of the ship against the current."

"And when the wheel was half over, were you able to see the compass?"

"Yes, sir."

"Had she changed her heading?"

"No, sir. She was still heading west by south, half south."

Aspinall nodded to Lord Mersey and stood up to approach the witness.

"Was the wheel ported any more?" he asked.

"Yes, sir."

"Who put the wheel over last?"

"I did."

"How much did you put it over?"
"Hard-a-port, sir."
"Who gave you the order?"
"I did it myself, sir."
"Without orders?"
"Yes, sir."
"Why did you do such a thing without orders?" Lord Mersey asked.
"I saw on the compass that the current was taking us over to the port side or left side."
"Have we been told before that the putting of the wheel hard-a-port was done by the witness?" Lord Mersey asked Aspinall and his fellow judges.
"It's certainly come as a great surprise to me," Aspinall said.
"After you had put the wheel hard-a-port, did you look at the compass?" Lord Mersey asked.
"Yes, sir. I was with the compass all the time."
"After the wheel had been put hard over, did you see any change in her course?"
"No. Not at all, sir. She was heading west by south, half south."
"After you had put her hard over, was any whistle blown by the *Storstad*?"
"Yes, sir. Two long blasts."
"Who pulled them?"
"I did, sir."
"And what did that mean?"
"That meant we were lying still."
"Do you think that was the cause of the collision, that you put the helm hard-a-port without orders from the navigating officer?" Aspinall asked.
"No, sir."

Aspinall sat down, looking very satisfied with himself. He had gotten Saxe to admit to hard-a-porting the vessel. It would have been a serious admission if it were not self-evident that the Norwegian vessel had to adjust its course to counter the strong tidal current in the St. Lawrence River.

Fifty-two

"What do you want, Galt? Haven't you caused enough trouble already?"

Galt had accompanied Godefroy and Françoise to the CPR office where they met with Peters, who was not at all happy to see them. Galt pulled over some chairs for Godefroy and Françoise and then sat down.

"I have some good news for you, Peters."

"It better be good," Peters said, as he put down his pen and pushed the account ledger aside.

"This is Mr Paradis and his daughter. Mr Paradis is a fisherman and was hired by the CPR in Rimouski to look for the bodies on the river."

"So, Paradis, have you been paid?"

"Yes, I have," Godefroy said. "I was paid by your man in Rimouski."

"Very good, then."

"That's not it, Peters," Galt said.

"Well, what is it then? Peters said, looking annoyed. "Spit it out."

"Mr Paradis found a man on the river, a survivor."

Peters fixed Galt with a look of incredulity.

"He was alive and floating on some debris, sir."

"So you think," Peters looked sceptical, "that this man

might be on our passenger list?"

"Yes, sir," Françoise said. "His name is Juvonen, Simo."

"From the name, we think he could be Finnish," Galt added.

"Where is he?"

"He's in Quebec. We're looking for him."

"What do you mean, you're looking for him?"

"We lost him in the crowd on the docks."

"Well, when you find the man, bring him in and we'll sort it out."

"Please, sir. Can you check the passenger list for the name?" Françoise asked.

Peters looked at the pretty girl and muttered something under his breath before he pulled out the list.

"Which class?"

"I would imagine 2nd or 3rd class," Galt said.

As Peters ran his finger down the list of names, Galt got up and squinted at the list over the man's shoulder.

"No, I don't see it," Peters said finally. "He's not on the list."

"Are you blind, Peters? You've got a 'Juven' right there under your nose," Galt said. "In fact, you've got two of them: a 'Simo' and an 'Arto'."

"The surname is not the same," Peters said as he turned to Godefroy and Françoise. "I'm afraid your man is not on the list."

"There's a mistake in the spelling," Galt insisted.

"We don't make mistakes in spelling, Galt. They copy the name from the passenger's ticket reservation."

"Don't be an arse, Peters. Your people misspell crew names all the time. You'd think they would take more care with passenger names, but they don't."

"Were the men rescued or lost at sea?" Françoise asked.

Peters sighed and peered at a note next to the names.

"One of them was. Arto was rescued. Simo was lost."

"He wasn't lost. We saved him," Françoise smiled, delighted by the news. "They must be brothers. Simo has a brother."

In a drawing room of the *Château Frontenac*, Sir Thomas Shea toasted Butler Aspinall and the CPR legal team.

"Cheers, gentlemen, and congratulations to Butler Aspinall here. You did a wonderful job. Saxe will be their downfall."

"Thank you, sir," Aspinall said. "You know it was a complete surprise, the porting of the helm."

"I think there will be a lot of long faces over there tonight," Walters said.

"It may take the wind out of the Galt episode, but I wouldn't say the war is over," Aspinall replied.

"And what does Lord Mersey think?" Shea asked.

Aspinall looked at Shea with a disapproving air.

"You can never tell with his Lordship. He keeps his own counsel, and his final report may hide some surprises."

"Well, drink up. I'm feeling quite confident tonight."

"The Canadian judges will have their opinions and his Lordship will respect them," Aspinall said. "I do think they will favour our side."

"I hope so, Mr Aspinall, I hope so. By the way, I have some other news. The Exchequer court has decided to seize the *Storstad* after refusing the bond offered by the owners."

"You think this could have a bearing on the case?" Aspinall asked.

"No, not really," Shea said.

"It does put some pressure on the other side," Walters

added.

"Of course it does," Shea said. "We filed for $2 million of damages, so the court is doing the right thing. The proceeds of the sale of the ship will be deposited with the court pending the final resolution. Let's just say that it bodes well for us."

After dark, Simo crawled out of the dusty alley, kicking a rat out of the way as he ran off. It was very late and he was afraid of the dark. He hurried along the dock and jumped onto the deck of a small freighter as he heard the sound of drunken voices coming his way. He climbed into one of its canvas-covered lifeboats and, rummaging around inside, found an old oilskin duster which he pulled over himself.

On the dock, he could hear loud voices as the men returned to their ships. The port area was geared to the needs of sailors and dock workers alike with its gambling houses, opium dens, brothels, grog-shops, tattoo parlours, and dance halls. The street was alive with activity until the early morning hours.

Simo crawled deeper into the lifeboat and thought of the Paradis family. He missed them, especially the free meals and the shots of whisky Godefroy gave him. Tomorrow, he would look for his brother in the city. Arto would take care of him.

Fifty-three

"How long have you been on the *Storstad*?"

"Thirteen months," stammered the quartermaster of the *Storstad*, Peter Johannsen, sitting in the witness box and replying to a question from Haight.

"And all that time as quartermaster?"

"Yes, sir."

"Were you at the wheel at the time of the collision with the *Empress*?"

"Yes, sir."

"When did you take the wheel?"

"Twenty minutes to three."

"What was your course before you ran into the *Empress*?"

"West by south, half south."

"Did you, before the collision, receive an order to change your wheel?"

"Yes, sir."

"What order was that?"

"Port."

"Who gave the order?"

"The chief officer."

"How far over did you put the wheel?"

"Half over."

"Did you put it over more later?"

"Hard over later."

"Why did you put it hard over?"

"The third mate came and put the wheel hard over."

"Before the third mate took the wheel, had the course of the ship changed any by compass?"

"No, sir."

"After the third mate put the wheel hard over, had the course changed?"

"No, sir."

"Mr Johannsen, at the time of the collision was the *Storstad* travelling fast or slow?" Lord Mersey asked.

"I do not know."

"A man at the wheel ought to know whether the ship has steerage way or not?"

"She had steering."

"When the mate put the wheel hard-a-port, did she answer?"

"No."

"Why not?" Lord Mersey asked.

"Too little headway."

Lord Mersey looked confused and glanced at Haight.

"I thought he told us just now that she had steerage headway."

"When the ship has speed ahead, she has steering, sir," Johannsen replied.

"If she had steerage way, and she answered quickly to her helm, why did she not answer on this occasion?" Lord Mersey asked.

"My Lord, I think the witness means that the ship did not have steerage way at the time of the collision," Haight said. "Mr Johannsen, how long before the collision did the mate put

the helm hard-a-port?"
"About one minute, sir."
"Did you see the *Empress* before the collision?"
"A little before the collision."
"On which bow was she?"
"The port bow."
"After the collision what became of the *Empress*?"
"I don't know. I had run aft and called the men."

Haight, Andersen, and Toftenes took a hansom cab outside the courtroom on St. Louis street to return to the ship.

"I cannot understand these questions," Captain Andersen said. "We make no secret. Every man knows that you cannot keep your heading against a tidal current when your engines are stopped."

"They are clutching at straws," Haight replied. "They want to make the most of this admission, which they know had no effect on the accident."

"'Clutching at straws'? What does it mean?" Toftenes asked, looking gloomily at Haight.

"It means they have very little to go on, Alfred."

"Saxe put the helm hard-a-port. It changed nothing, but it is important now I think," Toftenes said. "This is where the arrow strikes. This is our Achilles' heel, is it not?"

"No, Alfred. It's not so important. We are making a good case."

"I think so too, Mr Haight," Andersen said. "They are clutching at straws. It is good."

Toftenes looked unconvinced.

Fifty-four

The opium den was located in a nondescript building in the old port. Ashby entered the building accompanied by a constable and stopped a Chinese girl on the stairs.

"I'm looking for a Mrs Munro. Do you know her?"

The girl nodded and waved for Ashby and the policeman to follow her. She led them up the stairs.

"Does she come in here often?" Ashby asked.

"I know this name. She might be here," the girl said. "You can look in the rooms."

As the policeman waited on the stairs, Ashby followed the girl into a dark room where men and a few women were stretched out on low couches smoking long opium pipes. There were people from all walks of life. Two Chinese women moved about the room serving tea.

Ashby entered an adjoining room where a young girl was preparing an opium pipe for a client. He stopped to look at a man who appeared to be fast asleep. He recognized the man's face from the newspapers and moved on.

As Ashby left the room, Alfred Toftenes stirred briefly, lost in a world where there were no nightmares but only sweet dreams.

Galt joined Thomas and Françoise as they scoured the city, looking for their runaway. They entered the *Hôtel de la Plage*, an establishment opposite the docks that catered to sailors and ship staff. A young woman at the front desk looked up as they approached.

"We're looking for a man," Galt said. "He's Finnish, name of Juvonen."

The woman shook her head.

"He may have come by looking for his brother Arto?"

"Don't know this name, sir."

"Thank you, miss."

Galt joined Thomas and Françoise in the hall and together they left the hotel. They returned to their hansom cab. The driver whipped the horse, and they took off at a trot down the street.

"This fellow's not going to be easy to find," Galt said. "He sounds a bit off his head."

"Off his head?" Thomas asked.

Galt tapped his head, and Thomas nodded in agreement.

"You mean *'simple d'esprit'* I think," Françoise said.

"Yes, simple-minded."

"Do you think he would visit the hotels looking for his brother?" Françoise asked.

"I don't know, but that's what I would do if I was looking for my brother. They must have stayed a night or two in a hotel before embarking on the ship."

Ashby knocked on inspector Mainguy's door.

"Well, did you find her?" Mainguy asked, looking up from his desk.

"No, we went everywhere," Ashby replied, "I think Mrs

Munro is gone. She probably took a coach out of town."

"We'll keep looking. What about the husband's information about her opium habit?"

"She wasn't at the Chinaman's, Inspector. We checked."

"Suppose she decides to wait to see if her husband is released. He says he's innocent of all charges. He had nothing to do with the body snatch."

"She knows we're on to her. I don't think she would hang around. By the way, I did recognize someone over at the Chinaman's. Remember that Norwegian officer in all the papers? He was a witness at the inquiry."

"You mean the captain or the first officer?"

"The first officer, the blond guy. He was there."

"I know who you mean."

"Well, it looks like we've lost the enigmatic Mrs Munro, Inspector, at least for the time being."

"Don't worry, Ashby. We'll catch her sooner or later. I've notified the police in Peterborough that we're looking for her."

"I'll be at my hotel if you need me," Ashby said as he left the office.

Fifty-five

McLeod and Routhier were having their morning coffee in judges' chambers when Lord Mersey came in.

"So Routhier, what are the French papers saying about our inquiry?" Lord Mersey asked, pulling on his robe.

"The same thing the English papers are saying, sir," Routhier replied. "They're talking about Saxe's testimony."

The court clerk stuck his head into the room.

"Telegram for Lord Mersey."

McLeod collected the telegram from the clerk and handed it to Lord Mersey, who opened it.

"Ten minutes, sir," the clerk called to McLeod.

McLeod nodded to the clerk.

"Bloody hell," Lord Mersey bellowed. "Not another message from Douglas Hazen."

Lord Mersey read the message aloud.

"A BIRD IN THE HAND - SAXE."

He handed the telegram to McLeod, who looked at it.

"What does it mean?" Routhier asked, looking confused.

"It means a bird in the hand is worth two in the bush," boomed McLeod with a laugh.

"Of course, it does," Lord Mersey said.

"It means that Saxe is it," McLeod said. "We won't get a better admission of guilt than Saxe's testimony."

Lord Mersey turned to Routhier.

"*Un tiens vaut mieux que deux tu l'auras, n'est-ce pas*, Routhier?"

"Yes, I see it now. Thank you, sir," Routhier said.

"Bloody fool politician," Lord Mersey said in disgust. "Hazen can't help himself, just like that idiot Isaacs during the Titanic inquiry."

"Hazen will keep his nose out of it, sir," McLeod said, "but I agree with the minister that the Saxe testimony could be important."

"In affairs of state, gentlemen," Lord Mersey said, "my experience is that politicians put us all on a very short leash."

"You were the Marconi operator on the *Empress*?"

The Marconi operator, Ferguson, was in the witness box being questioned by Aspinall. He had been with the company for four years. He worked out of the wireless room at the back of the ship on the lower promenade deck.

"Yes, sir."

"Where were you when the *Storstad* slammed into the *Empress*?"

"On the starboard side. I saw her lights passing."

"How much of an impact was there when the ships hit?"

"Practically nothing."

"You saw the *Storstad* going astern?"

"Yes, that's right, sir."

"Did you see the *Storstad* long enough to know how she was heading at the time she went by?"

"I never saw the way she was heading. I just saw a blaze of lights passing the window. I immediately picked up the phone and called all stations and told them to stand by for a distress signal which I expected to be sent from the bridge."

"So what did you do?"

"I called up saying that we had struck something and were sinking fast. I sent it out very slowly because I knew that at the time there would be no senior operators on watch. Father Point replied saying "OK" and asking where we were."

"Where were you?"

"I remembered us putting down the pilot, so I said that we were about twenty miles past Rimouski. He then repeated 'twenty miles' wanting me to confirm it, to show that he had it right, and while I was saying yes, the power shut off and the lights went out. By this time, I was standing with one foot on the bulkhead and one on the floor. She was listing terribly. So I went out on the deck and shouted that there were plenty of ships coming."

The crew of *Storstad* was sitting down for their midday meal in the mess when John Griffin, the shipping agent representing the A.F. Klaveness line, arrived with two police officers.

"Hello, Mr Griffin. What can I do for you?" Captain Andersen asked.

"Captain, I'm sorry to disturb you during the lunch hour," Griffin replied. "I have some bad news. The government is seizing your ship. The papers arrived only this morning."

"Seizing the ship?" Andersen asked in disbelief as the crew broke out in agitated whispers.

"Yes, sir. As you know, the CPR and their underwriters are seeking a judgment against the Klaveness line for damages. The Exchequer court has decided to seize the asset, sir."

The senior constable stepped forward and read from a prepared statement.

"Our instructions are as follows, gentlemen. You have until tomorrow noon to collect your things and leave the ship. You are not allowed to remove anything of value, only your personal belongings. I hope this is clear."

"We cannot remain on board?" Andersen asked.

"No, sir. The company has reserved rooms for you in town until this thing blows over," Griffin said.

"But the inquiry is still going on," Frida said.

"Yes, and it will continue. This is just a precautionary move, Mrs Andersen," Griffin said.

"It seems very unusual, John. Why doesn't Klaveness provide a bond as a guarantee?" Andersen asked.

"We proposed a bond as security, but it was not acceptable to the Canadian government."

"So the government is going to sell the ship?"

"That seems to be the case, captain."

"Is the company going to find another ship for us?"

"At this stage, I really don't know."

The cook arrived with plates of food, but the men seemed to have lost their appetite.

Griffin pulled Andersen aside and whispered in his ear.

"Where's your first mate?"

"I don't know, John. I haven't seen him."

"He might be called again, you know. I heard that he was seen over at the Chinaman's."

Standing near her husband, Frida looked stricken.

"The men like to take the edge off," Andersen said. "Alfred has been under a lot of stress lately."

"You better find him quick and get him back here. He could be called at any time."

"Sure, I'll send a man over there to collect him after lunch."

Fifty-six

Thor was about to knock on the door to Captain Andersen's cabin when Frida appeared on the threshold, holding a box. She was busy cleaning out the cabin, ready for the move.

"We found him. He's still asleep," Thor said.

"Asleep?" Frida asked.

"We couldn't wake him. I left Fremmerlid there to collect him when he wakes up."

"Thank you, Thor."

"It's a pleasure, madam."

"We must take care of our own."

Thor nodded and was gone.

Frida knew about Toftenes' opium habits. He would often be gone for several days at a time in various ports and he was not the only man on board with the habit. Alfred was her cousin, so she felt responsible for him.

Galt entered the CPR office and noticed Peters filing papers.

"Oh, no. Not you again," Peters said, dropping a file.

"Mr Peters, how are you today, sir?" Galt asked.

"Look, Galt, I'm very busy. I need to get this done before Walters returns from his lunch break."

"I can see that, but we just need a wee bit of information.

You know the Paradis family is still looking for their man."

Peters collected the file from the floor and put it back on the desk.

"OK, what is it? Walters will be back very soon."

"The brother Arto Juvonen. Where's he staying?"

"God, I haven't got time for this."

"Come on Peters, all we need is the address."

Reluctantly, Peters put the files aside and pulled out the list of passenger accommodations provided by the CPR for the survivors and their families staying in the city.

"*Hôtel Belles Rives* on *rue St-Paul*."

"Thanks, Peters. I owe you one," Galt said with a grin.

"If you find the man, bring him around. We'll certainly look into it."

"Paradis wants to be paid."

"I'll talk to Walters."

"The family put him up in their house and paid for a doctor to see him. Not to mention bringing him here all the way from Rimouski."

Peters nodded as Galt left the office.

It was after dark when Galt, accompanied by Françoise and her brother Thomas, entered the lobby of *Hôtel Belles Rives* and stepped up to the front desk. An old man, impeccably dressed in a white shirt and waistcoat, came over to help them.

"Have you got a man by the name of Arto Juvonen staying with you, sir?" Galt asked.

"Yes, he went out about an hour ago," the clerk said.

"Can we wait here for him?"

"Of course, but I think he went to the church in *Place Royale* for the evening service, so you might catch him there."

Galt consulted with Thomas and Françoise briefly, and they left the lobby. They crossed the road and entered *Place Royale* with the *Notre-Dame-des-Victoires* church in the middle of the square.

The church had been named after the French victory over Sir William Phips in 1690 when the New Englanders had tried to take the city. The New England fleet was nearly destroyed by cannon volleys from the top of the cliffs. Later in 1759, the church had been almost completely destroyed by General Wolfe's cannons before the English forces took the city during the famous Battle of the Plains of Abraham.

The evening service was over, but several parishioners remained, either sitting in prayer or lighting prayer candles. Françoise noticed a man alone in one of the pews. She waited until he became aware of her presence and then approached.

"*Monsieur Juvonen?*"

"Yes," the man nodded.

Françoise waved for Galt and Thomas to come over.

"The man from the hotel told us we might find you here," Françoise said. "You are Arto Juvonen?"

"Yes, I am," the man said.

"Mr Juvenon, we've found your brother, sir," Galt said.

"Pardon me. What did you say?"

"Your brother, sir, Simo. He's alive."

Arto's eyes lit up as his expression was transformed from sorrow to joy in a fraction of a second.

"We arrived yesterday evening," Françoise said, "and just as we docked, Simo ran away."

"He does that from time to time," Arto said.

Françoise was sitting with Arto on an antique Victorian

loveseat with lace doilies in the lobby of the *Hôtel Belles Rives* opposite Galt and Thomas on hard-backed chairs. The hotel waiter brought them a tea service and put it on the table.

"He's a strange man," Françoise said, serving the tea.

"He's always been rather childlike. It's a condition that is caused by a lack of oxygen at birth. The German psychiatrist Eugen Bleuler calls it 'autistic thinking'. It means avoiding reality and living in a fantasy land."

"We thought you might be able to help us find him," Galt said. "You would know his favourite haunts in the city."

"Quebec is a big city, but I do have a few ideas of where he may have gone," Arto said. "He's afraid of the dark, so he won't be wandering around at night. He'll hide somewhere. We can start looking tomorrow."

"Once we find him, you'll need to go with Mr Paradis to confirm his identity at the CPR office," Galt said.

"My father needs to be paid, Mr Juvonen, for saving your brother and for bringing him to you," Françoise said.

"Don't worry, miss. If we find him, your father will be paid handsomely."

Fifty-seven

On the *Storstad*, Captain Andersen knocked on the door of the first mate's cabin in the early morning hours. Toftenes was half asleep as he opened the door.

"Alfred, how are you?" Andersen asked.

"I'm fine, sir," Toftenes said. "You were looking for me?"

"Dammit, Alfred. Your orders were to remain available, then you go off on a bender. What the hell are you up to?"

"I thought I was done, sir."

"Not necessarily. They can call you back at any moment. You need to get packed. We must leave the ship in a couple of hours."

"Where are we going, sir?"

"We're being put up in a hotel in town. Are you sure you're all right? You don't look very well."

"I'm fine, sir."

"Frida is worried about you. She thinks you should take better care of yourself."

"Yes, sir."

It was around nine o'clock that Alice entered the lobby of the Neptune Hotel on the waterfront. She went to the front desk and asked a young man with a thin moustache if James

Galt was there.

"I think he went out, miss," Pierre said. "Can I give him a message?"

Alice hesitated and then pulled a book out of her bag and put it on the counter.

"Do you have some writing paper, sir?"

Pierre pulled a sheet from the desk drawer and handed it to her along with a pen and ink.

"He'll be back soon, miss, if you want to wait."

"Thank, you."

Alice wrote in a neat cursive script with a practised hand, dipping the nib carefully in the ink, and then tucked the letter inside the book. She handed the book to Pierre and left the hotel. On the wooden sidewalk facing the waterfront, she called to a calèche just as James arrived on foot.

"Alice, what are you doing here?"

"Hello, James. I left a present for you at the front desk. I came by because I have a meeting with the police inspector tomorrow and was wondering whether you might accompany me."

"Of course, it would be a pleasure. What time?"

"Two o'clock at City Hall."

"I'll collect you at the rooming house, shall I?"

"That would be wonderful, James. Bye, now."

Alice climbed into a calèche and was gone. James returned to the hotel.

"Mr Galt, a lady left you a book and a note. Here it is."

Pierre handed him a copy of Joseph Conrad's *Heart of Darkness*. James peeked at the note inside and read:

Dear James,

I take my pen in hand to write you this short letter. Vicky has been asking about you. We enjoyed our day on the beach together.

I came by your hotel to give you a copy of this extraordinary novel by Joseph Conrad. It's an adventure story about a voyage up the Congo River in Africa. I found it sitting on a shelf at Mrs Pelletier's house. It was left behind by an English gentleman. I think you'll enjoy it. I also wanted to ask you to come with me to a meeting with the police inspector tomorrow at 2 o'clock. I don't want to go alone.
Very sincerely yours,
Alice

Around noon, John Griffin and a constable entered the *Storstad* to confirm the departure of the Norwegian crew. They ran into Captain Andersen coming out of his cabin with a bag.

"So captain, are all of you out?"

"Yes, I think I'm the last. I was collecting some things that Frida left behind."

Griffin and the constable had a look in the captain's cabin and then moved down the hall checking the officers' rooms one by one followed by the captain. The constable opened the door to Toftenes' cabin and found a battered seaman's chest with rope handles and brass fittings sitting on the floor near the door. He called to Griffin in the hall.

"There's a chest in here, sir."

Captain Andersen approached.

"That chest belongs to Alfred Toftenes, my first mate. I thought he had left already."

"Perhaps he forgot it, sir."

"I don't think so, he must still be on the ship somewhere."

An explosion was heard from the wheelhouse upstairs.

"That sounded like a gunshot," Andersen said as he ran up the stairs, followed by Griffin and the constable.

They arrived in the wheelhouse to find Toftenes lying in a pool of blood on the floor, a Luger handgun beside him. Andersen rushed to his side. He felt for a pulse and then started gingerly probing Toftenes' head with his fingertips.

"Is he dead?" Griffin asked.

"No, but he's shot off half his ear and the bullet grazed his skull," Andersen said, turning to the constable. "Get me some towels. There may be some left behind in the galley."

The constable rushed off to look for towels as Andersen pulled a clean handkerchief from his pocket and held it up against Toftenes' ear. The sharp pain caused Toftenes to come to his senses.

"What happened, Alfred?" Andersen asked.

Toftenes struggled to his feet in a daze with the captain's support. The constable returned with a dish towel and Andersen replaced the blood-soaked handkerchief with the towel which he wrapped around Toftenes' head.

"He says it was an accident," Andersen said to the constable. "The gun went off accidentally."

The constable picked up the Luger and examined the pistol as the captain exchanged a look with Griffin.

"Nice gun," the constable said.

"He's a lucky guy," Griffin said. "He'll have a scar, but I don't think there's too much damage."

"Yes, he's a lucky all right," Andersen said. "Alfred, try to hold the towel up against your ear to stop the bleeding. We better find you a doctor."

The captain helped Toftenes towards the door, leaving Griffin to deal with the constable.

Fifty-eight

A diver in a flexible canvas suit with a copper diving helmet was lifted from the deck of the *Marie Josephine* and swung out over the St. Lawrence. The conditions for the dive were ideal with a sunny day and little or no wind on the water. Slowly the man was lowered into the depths along with his air hose as the surface team watched nervously.

The salvage company had been hired by the CPR to recover the postal cargo, 212 bars of silver, and the purser's safe from the wreck of the *Empress*. The *Marie Josephine* was an old tramp steamer fitted with air compressors, valves, gauges and long lengths of hose. She had been towed to the wreck and moored to a gas buoy marking the site. A diver from the *HMS Essex* had already mapped the position of the hull on the bottom.

Near the wreck, the water was opaque, with strong tidal currents that frequently changed direction. The ship leaned to starboard at a 45-degree angle and the dive team feared that the ship would roll over at any moment. The water temperature hovered between two and three degrees above freezing, quickly numbing hands and fingers.

The divers' first task was to attach buoys to the forward bow of the ship, but they soon found themselves pulling bodies from the wreck and sending them up, hooked to lines to the surface.

Frida stepped out of Toftenes' hotel room and joined her husband in the hall.

"How is he?" Captain Andersen asked.

"The bleeding has slowed. The doctor is stitching up the ear. He'll be all right."

"He has said nothing since the accident."

Frida took her husband's arm and led him away down the hall out of earshot.

"You think he tried to top himself?" she asked.

"No doubt about it, Frida."

"Alfred comes from such an unhappy family, Thomas. His father and sister both took their own lives. Gunnar threw himself overboard one night..."

"He was drunk."

"You know better, Thomas. The crew thought it was a suicide. And there was no doubt about Kamilla. She gassed herself."

Frida glanced back at Alfred's room where the doctor was sewing up the mangled ear.

"We'll need to watch him day and night. He might try again."

"I know," Andersen nodded. "But for now, I thought it best to call it an accident. Griffin is handling it."

"Good. Let's keep it secret. Don't say a word to the crew."

"Of course, I won't."

"I have a little secret of my own, Thomas."

"What? What is it?" Andersen asked with concern.

"This isn't the time or place," Frida replied firmly.

"Come on, out with it."

"Are you sure you want to know?"

"Of course."

"I think I'm pregnant, Thomas. I haven't had my courses this month."

Andersen's face lit up with happiness. He took Frida in his arms and kissed her.

"That's wonderful, Frida! That's wonderful news. How long have you known?"

"I usually have them around the fifteenth. You remember we made love that night on the ship?"

Andersen looked at his wife with growing trepidation.

"I think the child was conceived on the night we ran into the passenger liner, Thomas."

"That's incredible!" Andersen said, clearly worried by the meaning of it.

"What?" Frida asked.

"To conceive a child on such a momentous night."

"I know it's hard to believe, but that's the only possible date. It's been almost a month."

Andersen was shaken.

"I'm going to have a baby, Thomas. We'll have a family."

"That's wonderful, Frida."

"I want to go home, to be with my mother and Agnes. I'm tired, I need a rest. I can't take this business with the ship anymore."

Andersen looked discouraged.

"I'll miss you."

Fifty-nine

"We have a man here, a Dr Weber, who is a specialist in forensic medicine. He's from Vienna and well known in his country. He may take an interest in your case. You should talk to him."

Alice and James looked hopeful as Mainguy lit his pipe in his office at City Hall.

"Do you think it will help?" Alice asked.

"You have nothing to lose. If you're interested in meeting this man, I will take you down."

"Down?"

"He works in the morgue, madam."

Alice and James exchanged a look, and Alice nodded at the inspector.

A few minutes later, they were sitting at a table in the autopsy room opposite *Herr Doktor Weber* sporting a large moustache and speaking with a strong German accent. In the background, a man was using a handsaw to cut through the chest cavity of a cadaver.

"You know forensic medicine has come a long way."

Assaulted by the odour of decomposing bodies and the rhythmic movement of the blade, Alice and James tried to focus all their attention on the doctor's words.

"We look at scars, bone fractures, blood types, dental

records, hair types. Yes, even hair can make an identification. A great deal of progress has been made through the recent work of Gustav Fritsch, a *sehr geehrter* colleague of mine in Vienna. With these techniques, we can identify most victims."

"Do you think you can help us with the identification of my son?" Alice asked.

"We can try, but we have many cases from the *Empress*. Several hundred bodies have not yet been claimed and many will go to their grave anonymously with no one to claim them. This is very sad."

Alice nodded.

"If you want me to do an analysis, I will need your complete collaboration."

"You can have mine, sir, but I do not know about the Thompsons."

"Why did you do it, Alfred?" Frida asked as she checked the bandage on his ear.

Alfred was lying on his bed in the hotel room.

"There's no point to my life, Frida. We're losing the case. It was my fault. I gave the order to Saxe."

"You are not responsible, Alfred. You mustn't blame yourself."

"It will be our downfall. I know it."

"Don't you worry yourself about the case. You only did your duty. The captain says so."

"I don't care anymore. I want to get away from here."

"That's a good idea, Alfred. Take some time off, go home for a while."

"I have no home. My parents are dead, my sister is dead."

"That's rubbish. Stop it. You're feeling sorry for yourself,

Alfred. You are not alone. You have me and my family. You have Agnes and young Niels."

Peters had gone for the day when First Officer Johnson barged into Walters' office.
"What do you want?" Walters asked.
"Well, I thought I'd come by and see how my old pal Walters was getting on," Johnson said, slurring his words.
"What do you want, Johnson?"
"How's the inquiry going? I hear it's not going so well. "
"You've been drinking, haven't you?"
"Yes, I have. I've been thinking about the case."
"Well, it would be going a lot better without Galt's testimony. He nearly sank our case, the bloody fool."
"Yes, sir, I saw it all in the papers. Well, Galt may not be your only problem."
"What are you talking about? Speak up, man."
"I'm starting to have my doubts about those bleedin' masthead lights. I may have been mistaken. You know how it is with one's memory. It comes and goes."
Johnson had finally gotten Walters' attention. The CPR superintendent looked like he was going to have a heart attack.
"Sit down, Johnson. Let's have a drink," Walters croaked as he pulled a whisky bottle and glasses from his desk drawer.
"Thank you."
Walters poured the whisky, and they clinked their glasses together.
"Cheers," Johnson said.
"Cheers. Ok, let's hear it."
"You remember my testimony about the two masthead lights?"

"Of course, I do. What of it?"

"I testified that I never saw the *Storstad's* green starboard light, and I didn't look at their masthead lights. Well, that is not entirely true. I was very busy, but I do recollect seeing the masthead lights, open on the port side of the *Storstad*, not the starboard side. I think that the captain was mistaken."

"Don't say another word," Walters said with a groan. "Not a word to anybody."

"Of course."

"Come back tomorrow. Let me have a talk with Shea."

Walters drank his whisky, weighing the potential harm Johnson's testimony could do to their case.

"You fellas drink only the best scotch, don't you, Walters?" Johnson said as he finished his glass and stood up.

"Please, take the bottle, Johnson. Thanks for coming in."

"It was a pleasure. See you tomorrow."

Johnson slipped the bottle into a canvas bag and left the office.

Sixty

"Miss Townshend, you were one of the passengers on the *Empress* at the time of the collision?"

"Yes."

Tiria Townshend had been called by Haight late in the day based on her replies to questions put to her by Mr Holden shortly after the sinking.

"You were awakened before the collision actually occurred?"

"I was awake sometime before the collision. I was awakened by the whistles. What whistles they were I do not know."

"How long was it after you were awakened by these whistles that you heard the three short blasts blown by the *Empress*?"

"That I could not tell you. It was some time."

"The whistles that woke you were not the signals of three short blasts?"

"Oh, no, certainly not."

"What were these whistles that woke you up?"

"The fog horn, sir. We were going through fog, whistling, going full speed ahead and then the other boat whistled in return."

"As I understand your statement to Mr Holden, you got up

and looked out the porthole and saw the fog?"

"I got up and looked out and could only discern the edge of the deck. The fog was very dense."

"When did you hear the signals of three short blasts blown twice?"

"Oh, that was sometime after I had been back in my berth."

"And after that, how did you manage to save yourself?"

"By the time I got out of the cabin with my aunt Wynnie, the ship was listing most frightfully. We got up onto the promenade deck and there was regular confusion. So we went up onto the boat deck. When she had listed so much it was impossible to stand, my aunt and I walked down the port side of the ship over the portholes. When the ship went down, we were thrown into the water."

"What happened to your aunt, Miss Townshend?"

"She disappeared in the fog, sir. I never saw her again."

"I'm sorry, miss."

Tiria Townshend wiped a tear from her eye with a handkerchief as Haight continued his questions.

It was dark in the reading room of the *Château Frontenac* as Walters approached Shea, comfortably ensconced in a leather armchair. Shea put down his newspaper and looked up at Walters, holding his bowler hat in his hand and looking defeated.

"What is it? What happened, man? Out with it!"

"Johnson is having doubts, sir. He says Kendall may be mistaken about the masthead lights on the *Storstad*."

"Damn! And I thought that things couldn't get any worse. Where is he?"

"He's coming around tomorrow. He wants a deal."

"Let me have a think about this."

"He's a key witness, sir," Walters said nervously. "If he goes to Haight and the Norwegians, we could be in trouble."

"Of course."

"You remember that he was in charge of the ship when Kendall went up the ladder to read the compass bearing. If he says the captain was mistaken..."

"Yes, I can see that."

"It would confirm the *Storstad* testimony that they were showing red, their port side light to the *Empress* before it disappeared in the fog."

"And the *Empress* was on a crossing course," Shea added.

"Yes, sir. It would explain the captain's order to put the engines astern to stop the ship because he feared a collision."

"Will it hurt our case?"

"I'm not sure, sir. I had a chat the other day with Captain Murray, the harbour master, about the inquiry. He's a smart man and has been following the case. I asked him hypothetically, of course, what would happen if the captain admitted to being mistaken."

"What did he say?"

"He said the *Empress* could be held responsible for the disaster because of rule 19, the one about crossing vessels."

"I thought the judges had decided that the rule didn't apply."

"Murray is not a lawyer, sir. You can check with Aspinall, but he thinks that, when there are crossing vessels, the rule does apply and the *Empress* was under the obligation to remove itself from the path of the *Storstad*."

"Damn, this could hurt our case. It could be worse than the steering gear testimony."

"I think so, sir."

"You know, Walters, if we lose this case, we are at risk for the loss of our ship, the damage to the collier, and, of course, the compensation for the horrendous loss of life. It could cost the company a fortune and damage our reputation for years to come."

"I realize the stakes are high, sir. You remember that the captain made no attempt to close the portholes and the watertight doors when he knew the ship was in imminent danger? That is sufficient to condemn us in the eyes of the judges."

Shea looked shocked by Walters' calm and rational explanation of the facts. He may have been a lowly superintendent in the company, but he had a wealth of experience in nautical matters.

"Bloody hell, Walters, don't say anymore. We must talk to Johnson as soon as possible."

Sixty-one

Galt, Arto, and Françoise arrived at the fairground, an open space dominated by a Ferris attraction with a *grande roue*. Nearby, there was a circus tent featuring exotic exhibits such as 'the bearded woman', 'the world's strongest man', and various knife and ball throwing competitions. A large crowd had gathered to watch a group of men throw baseballs at prizes on a shelf.

Galt and Françoise followed Arto through the crowd to the Ferris wheel where a queue of people was waiting. Arto went up to the bored attendant chewing gum.

"Sir, can you help us? We're looking for my brother. He's about my size, but he doesn't speak any English or French."

"Ain't seen 'im."

The attendant turned away, ignoring Arto, and pulled on a hand brake. The Ferris wheel slowed to a stop.

"He likes the Ferris wheel," Arto said. "We came here the day before we left Quebec."

"So you think he might come back?" Françoise asked.

"Yes."

Annoyed by the attendant's behaviour, Galt called out to him.

"Hey, mate," Galt yelled. "You seen a guy nosing 'round here, wanting free rides?"

"Yeah, I got one of 'em. I can't get rid of the arsehole. See that guy up there hiding in the bucket?"

They looked up into the sunlight and locked eyes with Simo, who climbed out of the bucket and started down.

"That's him. I can't get rid of the bastard. He keeps stealin' rides."

Arto rushed over to his brother.

"*Se olen minä.* It's me, Simo."

Simo stepped off the Ferris wheel, and Arto embraced him. He barely acknowledged his brother before his attention returned to the wheel.

As the attendant lunged for him, Simo slipped from his grasp and climbed the wheel like a monkey going to the top, hoping to catch another free ride.

"Son-of-a-bitch, he thinks he can do what he likes around here."

"I'm sorry, sir. I'll pay for his rides," Arto said to the attendant as he joined Galt and Françoise. "He's harmless, sir. He only wants to ride the wheel."

"We've found him," Galt said, "but how do we get him down from the wheel?"

"Don't worry. I'll catch him the next time the wheel stops."

"Mr Juvonen, I think it is not so easy," Françoise said, "to have such a brother."

"No, it's hard, but I'm so happy you have brought him back to me. He's the only family I have."

Judge Routhier, in his dressing gown, stepped out of his room with a towel over his arm, heading down the hall to maid service at the *Château Frontenac*. He passed a man in formal dress wearing a top hat and cloak coming toward him.

"Good evening, Judge," the man said.

Before Routhier had time to react, the man had passed him by and gone halfway down the hall to knock on Judge McLeod's door.

Routhier looked back and recognized the face puffing on a cigar as the person of Sir Thomas Shea, the railroad builder and president of CPR operations in Canada. He smiled at Routhier briefly before McLeod opened the door and ushered him inside.

Troubled by the encounter, Routhier continued on to maid service and returned to his room with a clean set of towels. He shut the door and went over to the desk in the corner. What Judge McLeod had just done was absolutely unacceptable and could lead to his resignation from the inquiry.

Judges were not allowed to hear cases in which they had any personal knowledge of the disputed facts, a personal bias concerning a party, or a financial interest in the case. They were to avoid impropriety of any kind and were simply not allowed to contact the parties. They were to observe the highest standards of conduct and maintain their independence and impartiality.

Routhier was furious with his colleague and felt let down. How could Judge McLeod permit such a thing? It was unthinkable. He started to compose a note to Lord Mersey on the hotel stationery. After writing for a minute or two, he stopped and tore up the letter, throwing it in the wastepaper basket. He stood up and paced the room.

Sixty-two

Godefroy and Thomas were stripped to the waist and perspiring as they cut into a large piece of driftwood using a crosscut saw on the deck of the *Rose des Vents*. It was hard work and Godefroy signalled for a break. He was mopping his face when he looked up at the dock and saw Françoise, Arto, and Simo approaching.

"*C'est merveilleux. Vous l'avez trouvé.* You've found our him!" Godefroy exclaimed.

Simo broke away from the others and leaped onto the boat, rushing over to hug Godefroy.

"Okay, Simo, okay. I'm happy to see you too," Godefroy said, holding the young man back.

"This is his brother, *Père*," Françoise said. "Arto Juvonen, this is my father."

"Mr Paradis. Thank you so much for saving Simo."

"Your brother gave us a scare, Mr Juvonen. A big scare," Godefroy said.

"We took him along to the CPR office," Françoise said. "The man said you can collect your bonus tomorrow, *Père*."

"That's very good news, *ma belle*. Can we offer you a cup of tea, Mr Juvenon, or perhaps something stronger?"

"Yes, I would like that."

Françoise headed to the galley to make the tea.

"You were one of the assistant stewards on the *Empress*?"
"Yes, sir."
The assistant steward Powell was in the witness box, being questioned by Newcombe. He was a nervous young man with sideburns and thinning hair.
"You were also a watchman on the night of the collision?"
"Yes, sir."
"What were your duties?"
"To light all the emergency lights in case of fog and to do other work."
"What was the other work?"
"Cleaning boots and such like."
"When the fog came on, did you light the lamps?"
"I was in the pantry. I lit the lamps after the collision."
"Did you know you were in a fog before the collision happened?"
"Yes, sir. I heard the fog horn once."
"You heard the fog horn of the *Empress* blow?" Lord Mersey asked.
"Yes, sir."
"How many blasts?"
"I heard one blast first."
Haight nodded at Newcombe and stood up to ask a question of the witness.
"How long before the collision was it that you heard her blow one blast?"
"I could not say exactly the time."
"About?"
"About ten minutes, sir."

"Did you hear her blow one blast several times?"
"I could not say, sir."
Haight sat down to allow Newcombe to continue.
"After the collision, what did you do?"
"I ran through the salon and the chief watchman told me to call all passengers and get their lifebelts on. As I went on, I lit four emergency lamps."

Arto, Godefroy, and Françoise lounged on the deck in the late afternoon sunshine as Thomas helped Simo fish for perch from a line off the deck. He had already caught several small ones while the men drank their whisky and talked.

"So what do you do for a living, Mr Juvonen?" Godefroy asked.

"I'm a geologist," Arto said. "My job is to look for metals in the earth: iron, gold, silver, copper. Simo and I came from Marquette on Lake Superior."

"*Le lac Supérior*?"

"Yes. There are a lot of iron mines in Michigan, Mr Paradis. I was doing exploration work there for three months. I have an uncle who lives in Marquette. We were on our way home."

"I hear that Lake Superior is a very big lake."

"It's an inland sea, Mr Paradis. A huge lake. We sailed from Marquette to Buffalo on Lake Erie and then took the train."

"How were you separated from Simo?"

"On the night of the disaster, Simo couldn't sleep, so we played games until late. We hadn't gone to bed when we heard the whistles, so we immediately went up to the boat deck to have a look. We were lucky to get there at all. It was quite a struggle with the listing of the ship. Then everything happened very fast. I was putting on my life jacket and watching a boat being lowered into the water. When I turned around, Simo had disappeared. I looked everywhere for him."

Sixty-three

A rough-looking man with a scraggly goatee was in the witness box, being sworn in as Haight glanced at his notes. He stood up and approached the witness.

"You were the boatswain's mate on the *Empress*, were you not, Mr Radley?"

"Yes, sir."

"So you were in charge of the lifeboats, the rigging, the anchors, the deck? Is it a big responsibility?"

"Yes, sir."

"Where were you when the collision occurred?"

"On the forward well deck, the upper steerage deck."

"Were you on the deck when the fog first shut in?"

"Yes."

"What was the first signal that you heard?"

"The first that got my attention was the three short blasts. I don't take notice of an ordinary fog signal when I'm working on the deck."

"Do you remember hearing some whistles blown by the *Empress* before you heard the signal of three blasts?"

"Yes, I do."

"Is it not true that the first signal you heard from the *Empress* was one long blast?"

"Very likely."

"Mr Holden has been good enough," Haight referred to his notes, "to give me the statement you made to him in the first instance. You stated to him that the first signal you heard from the *Empress* was a signal of one long blast?"

"Yes."

"This is the statement you made to him shortly after the accident?"

"Yes, very soon after."

"What was the first light that you saw from the *Storstad*?"

"Her masthead lights."

"Did you see any of her coloured lights?"

"I saw both of them, but I noticed the red one more."

Aspinall stood up to ask a question and Haight allowed him to go ahead.

"Did you hear any other blasts from the *Empress*?" Aspinall asked.

"I heard two long blasts."

"What is the significance of the blasts that you are referring to?"

"Two long blasts would indicate they were stopped."

Lord Mersey turned to the lawyers.

"Can you tell me why this evidence has not been called till so late in the case?" Lord Mersey asked, looking annoyed. "It seems to me to be important. How is it that this statement comes at the last moment?"

"I'm sorry, sir," Newcombe said from his seat at the table, he shared with Aspinall and Haight. "There has been a bit of a mix-up with our witnesses."

"This witness, at some time or another shortly after the disaster, made the statement that the first whistle that he heard from the *Empress* was a long blast," Lord Mersey said. "That seems to me to be important since Captain Kendall clearly testified that no such blast was blown. So it is important to ascertain whether there was such a blast or not."

"I have a copy of the statement the witness made to Mr Holden," Haight said as he passed the document to Lord Mersey, who examined it.

"You clearly say," Lord Mersey said after reading the document, "that the *Empress* blew fog signals two or three times before going astern. Do you agree with the statement, Mr Radley?"

"Yes, sir."

"And the fog signal. What do you mean by a fog signal?"

"A single blast, a single long blast, sir."

Sixty-four

Inspector Mainguy had called in both parties in the Thompson vs. Bingham affair. Alice arrived with Pauline and sat opposite Mr Thompson, who had come alone. His wife had refused to be in the same room as Alice. Mainguy stood near the door while Dr Weber occupied his desk.

"Ladies and gentlemen," Weber began. "I have examined the facts in this case. It appears that the hair samples provide the most conclusive evidence. If you look at hair under the microscope, it is very different from one head to another. I look for clues, just like my detective friend here. I examine the thickness, the medulla size and the colouration of the hair cortex. My colleague, Gustav Fritsch in Vienna, has studied hair samples from Germans, Lithuanians, Poles, Italians, and others to identify the various types of hair. For instance, it is possible to distinguish Lithuanian hair from many German types. You are impatient to know what I find?"

The others nodded expectantly.

"The boy has very fine hair, very unusual hair for a boy of English heritage. The thickness, density and colouration are very different."

Alice looked puzzled.

"There is no doubt in my mind, Mrs Bingham, that the boy cannot be your son."

Alice gasped in dismay.

Weber turned to Thompson: "nor can he be yours, I'm afraid, Mr Thompson."

Thompson looked dumbstruck. Pauline held Alice's hand as tears welled up in her eyes.

"We have found that the boy is the son of a Polish immigrant travelling in 3rd class. We have a positive match on the hair. The man was lucky to survive, but lost his wife and child in the disaster."

"Oh, God," Alice said, standing up. "This is terrible. I'm so ashamed."

"I'm sorry, Mrs Bingham," Thompson said. "I had no idea. I don't know how I will tell my wife."

"It's for the best," Weber continued. "We need to put the child with the right parents."

Thompson left quickly, nodding politely to both Dr Weber and the inspector.

"How could I make a mistake like this?" Alice asked Pauline.

"It's not your fault, my dear," Pauline said in a comforting tone. "You wanted to believe."

They stood up and headed for the door.

"Thank you, Dr Weber," Pauline said. "Thank you, Inspector."

"I heard the news from the police inspector. How is she?" James had just come in and was standing in the hall.

"She's terribly upset," Pauline said as she ushered James into the parlour. "Please help yourself to a brandy, Mr Galt. There are some glasses in the cabinet. I'll fetch Alice."

"Thank you, madam."

James found the glasses and poured the brandy. After a moment, Alice came down wearing her dressing gown, followed by Pauline.

"Alice, let's have a drink. It will do you both good," Pauline said, as she sat in the corner with her knitting.

James passed around the glasses, and they sat in silence until Alice spoke.

"You never told me how it was for you on the ship, James?"

James looked up, surprised by the question.

"I was having a smoke on the forward deck when we struck the collier. It was very strange, seeing that ship come at us out of the fog. There was hardly any shock at all. Just the crunch of metal plates buckling and tearing."

"Then what did you do?"

"I ran to my station, and we were sent down to examine the bulkhead where the flooding was worst and to close as many watertight doors as we could. The stokers were climbing out of the hatches with the water coming in fast behind them. We saved a lot of men, but some drowned in the breached boiler rooms."

Alice's thoughts returned to the listing ship.

"We returned to the boat deck to help put the boats in the water. It was total chaos up there, as you know."

Alice looked at James and took his hand in hers.

"When the ship went down," James continued, "I jumped into the water as close as I could to a lifeboat. I suppose I was lucky that the ship didn't drag me down, as it did many of my friends."

Captain Kendall stood at the window in the dining room of the Neptune Hotel and watched a man in a dark suit and fedora standing across the street. The man seemed to be waiting for something to happen and hadn't moved for some time.

"This isn't your usual style, Henry."

Kendall turned from the window to see Johnson standing in the doorway.

"You must miss the luxurious accommodation at the *Château*," he said as they shook hands. "So, how have you been?"

"There's a man watching the hotel."

"It must be one of Walters' men keeping an eye on you. They don't want you running off again."

"That's quite outrageous. I've finished with the inquiry."

"Well, you know Walters. He's about as suspicious as they come."

Johnson poured himself a cup of tea from the pot on the stove and sat down at the table.

"I mentioned my faulty memory to Walters," Johnson said. "Shea says he's going to make me an offer."

Kendall frowned at Johnson.

"You are not to judge me, Henry. I'm only asking for my due."

The captain refrained from commenting, knowing that any remark might set off Johnson.

"A captain with an extra-master certificate. What a bloody fraud you were!" Johnson exclaimed with bitterness. "I remember how perfect you were, the way you talked to the men, up there on the bridge with the bloody natives down below. To think that I wanted to be like you. Now, you're nothing, you're washed up just like the rest of us."

Johnson laughed and pulled out a flask of whisky from his pocket. He poured a shot into his tea.

"So how much do you think my testimony is worth, Henry? I was on the bridge. I saw it all."

"Yes, you saw it all," Kendall said, keeping one eye on the man in the street.

"I'll tell them everything."

Kendall nodded, looking grim.

"You think they'll call me?"

"I have no idea, Edward."

Sixty-five

"Who killed Cock Robin?
I, said the Sparrow,
with my bow and arrow,
I killed Cock Robin."

"Jamie loved Cock Robin," Alice said. "It was his favourite. He'd often get the giggles with the animal voices."

James and Alice were sitting in the parlour, drinking brandy while Pauline was knitting in the corner. Alice recited the words of the nursery rhyme by heart.

"Who saw him die?
I, said the Fly,
with my little eye,
I saw him die."

"Who caught his blood?
I, said the Fish,
with my little dish,
I caught his blood."

"Who'll make the shroud?

*I, said the Beetle,
with my thread and needle,
I'll make the shroud."*

"Who'll dig his grave?
*I, said the Owl,
with my little trowel,
I'll dig his grave."*

"Jamie loved the 'little eye' and the 'little trowel'. He would crack up whenever I mentioned them."

"What a wonderful boy," Pauline said, wiping a tear from her eye.

"'It goes on and on but finishes with a sad lament.'"

*"All the birds of the air
fell a-sighing and a-sobbing,
when they heard the bell toll
for poor Cock Robin."*

"Jamie was always sad when he heard the bell toll."

Alice closed her eyes for a moment.

"When Tom and I got to the upper deck, we waited near the lifeboats. Tom had found two life jackets, one for Jamie and one for me. Already the ship was listing terribly, and we were bracing with our feet on the rail."

"Alice, don't!" James said.

"*C'est une histoire terrible*, Alice," Pauline said.

"I want to tell it. I must," Alice insisted. "I abandoned my husband and child."

"Nobody thinks that," James said.

"I think about it all the time. What kind of woman would do

that?"

"But you didn't abandon them!"

Alice closed her eyes and relived those terrible moments.

Alice and Jamie sat perched on the railing, looking down at the lifeboat in the water. Several dozen people had jumped into the water in desperation. Tom crawled over to Alice and Jamie with the two lifebelts under his arm.

"Alice put this on."

"But I can swim, Tom. You put it on."

"Do it now. I'll hold Jamie."

Alice slipped into the lifebelt while Tom put his arms around Jamie and the railing. The ship suddenly gave a sharp jerk to starboard and Alice lost her balance, slipping off the railing into the water below, leaving her husband and child to fend for themselves.

"When I came to the surface," Alice said, "I could see my Jamie at the railing, but Tom was nowhere in sight. Then the *Empress* rocked one final time and went down. I couldn't see either of them in the water. I abandoned them."

"Stop it, Alice," insisted James. "I was there. There was nothing you could have done to save them. No one could."

"I found some floating debris and held on for dear life," Alice continued. "It was so dark and cold in the river. I managed to pull myself up onto this wooden crate. In the morning, I found myself washed up on the beach."

James looked down at his hands. He thought about Alice's nightmarish experience. Would she ever get over this tragedy? Some people never recover from such horrific experiences. They remain a stain on the rest of their lives. Alice was tough and resilient, but would she get over the loss of her son and husband? Would she become just another victim of the passenger liner - one of so many shipwrecked lives?

Sixty-six

"Gentlemen, you are bidding on the collier *Storstad* with a damaged bow," the judge announced in the small Admiralty court. "In its present state, the ship is in no condition to leave these waters and will require substantial repairs. The court has fixed initial bidding at $100,000."

Captain Andersen and Frida sat at the back of the room. The judge and several court employees sat behind the dais while a crowd of potential buyers sat on benches in front.

"I believe we are ready to start the bidding," the judge nodded at the auctioneer as he made his way to the front.

"Do we have any bids?" the auctioneer asked.

"Where's our man?" Frida whispered to her husband.

"That's him in the front row, Mr Cornell. He works for the Klaveness line."

A man held up his hand.

"OK. We have a bid here for $100,000," the auctioneer said. "Another in the back there for $105,000."

"What's Mr Cornell doing?" Frida said.

"He's waiting to see where the price will go," Andersen whispered. "Don't worry, he knows what he's doing."

"Do we have a bid for $110,000?" the auctioneer asked the crowd. "Yes, we have $110,000."

The men on the *Marie Josephine* had hauled their diver almost to the surface when they realized that something had gone terribly wrong. The heavy diving gear didn't permit much movement, but their man, an expert diver from New York named Edward Cossaboom, appeared totally lifeless as they pulled him onto the deck in his copper diving helmet and flexible canvas suit.

Even as the team rushed to remove the copper helmet, they knew their diver was dead, a victim of the 'squeeze' that had claimed so many lives in this dangerous profession. The men on the boat had no way of knowing that Cossaboom had lost his footing on the boat deck and had fallen to the muddy bottom of the river. The squeeze occurred when the air pressure in the suit was not properly adjusted to the exterior water pressure. The fall to the river bottom had substantially increased the water pressure on his suit, which had collapsed the flexible canvas suit and pushed the blood volume of his arms and legs into his heart and lungs until his chest literally exploded.

It was a terrible tragedy for the dive team. They had spent several days charting the position of the wreck on the bottom, which meant crawling along the length of the ship from stern to bow. Access to the wreck had to be through deck hatches on the port side, as she was leaning too much to starboard. The tidal currents and the opacity of the water made the work on the wreck exceedingly dangerous. It was simply impossible to reach the wreck when the current was running at peak flow.

After the death of Cossaboom, the men returned to work. The passageways inside the wreck were crammed with hideously disfigured corpses. The divers had to pull them out one at a time and hook them to lines for the trip to the surface. In total, eighty-eight bodies were removed from the ship by the divers.

It was not possible to remove all the bodies from the wreck, several hundred would remain entombed within the hull forever. Most of the bodies were too far gone to be identified and ended up in a mass grave at *Pointe Pouliot* in Rimouski, Quebec.

Sixty-seven

"Do we have a bid for $168,000?" the auctioneer asked.

There was silence in the courtroom. Frida looked around the room.

"We have a bid from Mr Thomas Hall here for $168,000. What about you gentlemen in the back there?"

The tension mounted among the bidders as Frida grabbed her husband's arm.

"What's he doing?" Frida asked in a whisper. "He's going to lose it."

"We have a bid here for $168,000 from Mr Hall. Do we have any other bids?"

A murmur went through the room.

"All right, we have a bid here of $168,000. Going, going,..." Cornell held up his hand.

"Mr Cornell, do we have a bid, sir?"

"$175,000."

"Excellent, sir. Do we have any other bids?"

The auctioneer looked around the room for other bidders.

"Mr Hall? Gentlemen? We have a bid here of $175,000. Any more bids?"

The auctioneer paused for a moment.

"OK, gentlemen. We have a bid of $175,000 for the ship. Going, going, gone. The ship is sold to Mr Cornell for

$175,000."

Andersen grinned at Frida.

"I knew he'd get it."

"We have our ship back," Frida said delighted by the outcome.

"Mr Reinertz, you were the second officer on the *Storstad* at the time of the collision with the *Empress of Ireland*?

"Yes, sir."

The second officer with a large beard and glasses sat in the box being questioned by Haight.

"How long had you been on the *Storstad*?"

"I joined in Sydney, Nova Scotia."

"How long have you been going to sea?"

"About 12 years."

"What papers have you?"

"A master's certificate."

"Where were you at the time of the collision?"

"I was sleeping when the collision occurred."

"Was it the jar of the collision that woke you?"

"Yes."

"Where did you go when you felt the collision?"

"I went to the boat deck."

"On which side?"

"The starboard side of the boat."

"When you reached the boat deck, could you see anything of the other steamer?"

"Yes, sir. I saw the lights of the *Empress* going from the port bow over to the starboard bow. It was moving fast."

"What?" Lord Mersey asked.

"The *Empress* was moving fast."

"Am I to understand that this was after the collision?"
"Yes."
"You saw the *Empress* was moving forward?"
"Yes."
"Could you tell anything about the angle in which the vessels were lying when you got up?" Haight asked.
"No, sir."
"Did you receive any orders from Captain Andersen?"
"Yes, to lower the boats."
"What boats did you handle yourself?"
"Starboard no. 2."
"Were the boats cleared and the men standing by when you got the order?"
"Yes, they were standing by. I heard the cries of the *Empress* people and we lowered the boat at once."
"How far was the *Empress* from the *Storstad* as you rode from your vessel towards the sinking steamer?"
"About two ship lengths."
"How many people did you pick up in your boat on the first trip?"
"I rescued about 50 people on the first trip."
"What was the capacity of your boat?"
"About 30. We were overloaded because we had to save as many people as possible. People were crying out not to take any more, but we had to take as many as we could because there was not a moment to lose."
"You returned to the *Storstad* and then went back a second time, did you not?"
"Yes, I did."
"Had the *Empress* gone down before you got back the second time?"
"She had gone down when I was leaving on my first trip."

"How many people did you get on the second trip?"
"About 13."
"Did you make a third trip?"
"Yes, I found some passengers standing on a boat and one man, half dead, lying on the boat. He was picked up."
"Did you pick up any dead bodies?"
"Yes, we did, sir."

Sixty-eight

There is a narrow path with a view of the river leading from the Plains of Abraham down toward the *Château Frontenac*. On one side, the cliff face drops down some fifty metres to the river and the streets of the lower town. Toftenes led the way, followed by Captain Andersen and Frida walking arm in arm.

"So when do you want to go?" Andersen asked.

"I want to leave in two weeks, so I can catch up with Agnes and Niels," Frida said. "They may be too much for my mum. You know how she is."

"Can't you let Agnes fend for herself a bit? She made her bed, now she must lie in it."

"Agnes is not so strong, Thomas. There'll be a lot of shaking of heads and murmuring voices about how a married woman should never abandon her man. She'll need my support."

"We're going to lose most of our crew with the delays and the half pay. Saxe is leaving for Halifax on the train with several of the men. It's going to take a couple of months to repair the ship and then we'll be understaffed. I'll need you here."

Frida stopped suddenly when Toftenes jumped up on the rampart overlooking the lower town.

"Alfred, please get down from there," Frida said. "You make me nervous."

Andersen approached Toftenes, who seemed fixated on the road below. *The height was clearly sufficient. One foot over the edge and he would be gone in a fraction of a second. A quick end to a useless life.* He turned and smiled at Frida.

"You promised me, Alfred, you promised!" Frida said in desperation, fearing he might jump.

Andersen inched closer in the hope of grabbing his arm.

"You know I never told you the whole truth about that night on the ship," Toftenes said.

"You told us enough, Alfred," Andersen said.

"I told the lawyers the facts as I knew them. What we saw, what we did, not what we felt. The inquiry was only interested in the facts of the case, not in the real story."

"The real story?" Andersen asked, looking annoyed. "What are you talking about?"

"I had a premonition that something was wrong when we first entered the fog."

"You did what you had to do, Alfred," Frida said.

"We saw their red, port side light just before the fog shut us out so we went for a right-hand passage. When the *Empress* blew her three whistles, I knew something was wrong. If you are confident about your position, you don't stop your ship. You slow down and maintain course."

"What else could you do?" Andersen said.

"I simply followed the rules of navigation. We slowed, we maintained course. That was a big mistake."

"That was no mistake, Alfred."

"It was a mistake because I knew that the *Empress* had not intentionally shown its port side. It came around very slowly, revealing red over several minutes before the fog shut it out."

"There you have it, Alfred."

"The *Empress* is a fast ship. She was going 17 knots and

when you bring the helm to port, the ship comes around quickly. It doesn't slowly drift from green to red, particularly if you are heading towards another vessel with a fog coming in. You need to make your intentions clear. That should have told me they had no intention of going for a right-hand passage."

"But Alfred, you cannot know what went through their heads."

"I felt that a red-to-red passage was wrong. I should have changed course and headed due north to get us out of the fog."

"That would have been against company policy. I would have had to make a report."

Toftenes jumped down off the rampart and Frida sighed with relief.

"A report," Toftenes said in a mocking tone. "Who gives a damn about company policy and reports when lives are at stake?"

"Who have you talked to about this?"

"Saxe, I mentioned it to Saxe, but he doesn't believe it."

"And neither do I."

"We followed the rules and look what happened. We ran our ship halfway through the *Empress* midsection. She came out of nowhere and cut across our bow. If we had seen her a minute or two earlier, we could have turned our ship and slammed into her on our starboard side, causing some damage but no loss of life."

"Listen to me, Alfred. You are in a slow-moving collier going against the current and there is this huge passenger liner racing towards you at twice your speed in a fog. You can do nothing. You can only pray and hope to stay out of its way."

"I could have done better," Toftenes said. "I should have done something! On the water, the rules can get you killed."

He turned away and continued down the narrow path.

"He's right, you know," Frida said as they followed Toftenes down the path.

"That's the craziest idea I ever heard," Andersen said. "In all my time at sea, I never heard such bloody nonsense."

"Did you notice something?" Frida said.

"No. What?"

"Alfred smiled. I think he's feeling better. He's going to be all right."

Andersen looked at his wife with consternation.

Sixty-nine

"Mr Hillhouse, as a naval architect familiar with the design of the *Empress* ships, is it not true that the broad stern on these ships tends to cause eddies and has an effect upon the rudder?" Haight asked.

"Yes."

The naval architect in the witness box was a distinguished-looking older gentleman, with a moustache and mutton chops.

"Is it not true that after the *Empress* was first built, you found some difficulty with the rudder as originally designed?"

"On the trials of the vessel, everybody was absolutely satisfied with her steering qualities. Sometime later the fore part of the rudder got carried away and when that was being renewed, advantage was taken to increase the area of the rudder."

"Is it not true that the reason for increasing the area of the rudder was because a complaint had been made that the *Empress* did not steer well?"

"The reason, as I understand it, was that they wanted to improve her steering qualities," Hillhouse said.

"Will you please tell me when that change in the rudder was made?"

"In 1908, I believe."

"And was a similar change made to the rudder of the *Empress of Britain*, her sister ship?"

"Yes, I think so."

Lord Mersey leaned forward to ask a question.

"Mr Hillhouse, before the alterations on the rudder were made, had you heard complaints from the masters of either of the two ships?"

"No, but since the owners desired the change, I assume that they thought her steering might be improved."

Haight continued his questions.

"Captain Kendall has testified, Mr Hillhouse, that in his judgment when the *Storstad* struck the side of the *Empress*, she actually rebounded like a ball striking water. With your knowledge of ship construction and of moving forces, is this possible?"

"No, I do not think so."

"The forward movement of the *Storstad* is absolutely taken up in the crushing in of her own bow and the crushing in of the side of the *Empress*."

"Yes."

"From the examination, which you have made, how far do you think she penetrated inboard from the side of the *Empress*?"

"About 18 feet. That is partly from an examination of the *Storstad* herself and measurements of the model."

Haight held up the plaque for cabin number 328.

"The *Storstad* crew found this plaque from cabin number 328 on their vessel after the collision. Is room 328, Mr Hillhouse, almost in the exact centre of the *Empress*, calculating from stem to stern?"

"Yes, I believe it would be very near, almost exactly in the centre."

"Now, if the *Storstad* strikes the *Empress* at an angle, as indicated by Captain Kendall opposite room 328, would there be any tendency to swing the stern of the *Empress* one way or the other?"

"No, I think not."

"After the *Storstad* entered the side of the *Empress*, the *Storstad* was observed to have swung to starboard and then to have disappeared in the fog astern. To what do you attribute such movement of the two vessels?"

"Well, that might have been caused by the *Storstad* going astern with her rudder over or it might have been caused by a head motion on the *Empress*."

"I will ask you to assume that when the *Storstad* struck the *Empress*, the instant that she struck, the engines were put ahead. The ships then separated almost in a parallel position. In your opinion, Mr Hillhouse, could anything but the movement of the *Empress* explain such a position?"

"I think not if the *Storstad*'s engines were kept going ahead. The *Empress* must have had head motion on her at the moment of the collision and swung the *Storstad* into a parallel position."

Frida left the hotel on *rue St-Paul* on the arm of Alfred Toftenes. He was clutching a shabby briefcase and looked pale in his officer's uniform. Captain Andersen followed them out towards a large, four-wheeled hansom cab where the driver and the bellboy were loading Toftenes' sea chest.

Frida climbed on board first, followed by Toftenes who sat opposite her. Andersen sat next to his wife and signalled to the driver to depart. The cab lumbered along the waterfront to the ferry for Levis.

"Mr O'Donovan, you were one of the engineers on the *Empress of Ireland*, weren't you?"

"Yes, sir."

The young man with a dark complexion and black beard was taking questions from Newcombe in the witness box.

"At the time of the disaster, you were in the stoke?"

"Forward stoke, sir."

"Can you tell us what happened? What was the first thing you felt?"

"After the impact, about 20 seconds after, water rushed through the starboard No. 2 bunker into the stokehole."

"That is on the starboard side of the ship?" Lord Mersey asked.

"Yes, my Lord."

"How far below the water are these stokeholes?" Newcombe asked.

"I would think about 15 feet."

"Was the water coming in fast?" Lord Mersey asked.

"Yes, a great body of water, the full volume of the door."

"What happened next, after you saw this great body of water flooding in?"

"When I saw the amount of water rushing into the stokehole, I ordered all the firemen out."

"Otherwise, they would have drowned?"

"They would have if they had stayed there, my Lord."

Seventy

Captain Andersen and Frida waved goodbye to Toftenes as the Halifax train pulled out of the station.

"When will he get in?" Frida asked.

"Tomorrow," Andersen said. "Saxe will pick him up at the station in Halifax."

"Do you think he'll be all right?"

"He craves the work, Frida. We don't want him sitting around here doing nothing."

"Do you think he has changed?"

"Changed?"

"Yes, I think he is more light-hearted."

Andersen looked at his wife.

"I think he smiles more because of the company he keeps. You've spent a lot of time with him, my dear."

Frida laughed.

"Yes, I have. I try to keep up his spirits and chase away the dark thoughts, Thomas."

"You've done very well, Frida. If anyone can change him, you can. I told Saxe to keep an eye on him. Their ship is arriving in Halifax later in the week."

"Well, he does like Saxe and Johannsen, they are good friends."

"It's for the best, my dear."

"Have you just come from the scene of the wreck, sir?"

"Yes, I arrived this morning."

William Wotherspoon, a professional diver with the American Salvage Company, was in the witness box. He was a rough-looking man with mutton chops and a sunburn. He was taking questions from Newcombe.

"You were in charge of the diving operations?"

"Yes, sir."

"Most unfortunately, you lost your principal diver there the other day?"

"One of them, sir."

"What is your engagement in regard to the *Empress of Ireland*?'

"First to get the bodies out, then the mails and a quantity of silver."

"You were engaged by the CPR to make every effort possible to recover the bodies that are still in the boat?"

"Yes, sir."

"By the Postmaster General to recover the mails and by the insurers to recover the silver bullion?'

"Quite right, sir."

"So your diver went down to make a survey of the position of the wreck?"

"Yes, he went down intending to find the stern of the vessel and put a mooring line on it. We believe he lost his life by sliding down the forecastle head and severing his air hose. The vessel has a terrible slant to her side."

Haight stood up to ask a question of the witness.

"Your divers fixed two moorings to the ship, did they not? Where are they fixed?"

"One was made fast to the stern of the ship and the other

near hatch no. 4."

"And the forward bow?"

"The forward bow was not made fast by him, but a chain was put down to the forecastle head and one of the jib stays was made fast."

"What is the line of these buoys?"

"The position of the vessel lies roughly northeast to southwest by compass."

"Northeast the bow and stern southwest?"

"Yes, sir."

"The bow northeast?" Lord Mersey asked.

"Yes, sir."

"That being the direction in which she was travelling when she sank?"

"Yes, sir."

Mr Aspinall stood up to ask a question.

"As you get down towards the bed of the river, do the currents run very swiftly?"

"There is a two-and-a-half knot current running in the same direction at the top and bottom."

"When you get towards the bottom, the current does not necessarily run in the same way as the current at the top?"

"Towards the middle of flood or ebb, it probably runs the same way top and bottom, but as the tide changes, it changes at the top first."

"Then a vessel sinking might have its heading affected?"

"Yes, sir. It's possible."

Mr Haight stood up to ask a question.

"The tide tables on the night of the disaster show low water at 10 p.m. and high water at 4 a.m."

"Yes, sir."

"So the collision happened around halfway between flood

and ebb, and the movement of the water would have been about the same at the top and the bottom, would it not?"

"Yes, it would appear to be the same. Of course, there is an eddy where the shoreline forms a sort of sweep at that point and the tide does not run directly up and down the river."

Lord Mersey looked annoyed.

"Mr Haight, I have listened to your questions. Can you tell me quite simply what the evidence is supposed to establish?"

"That the bow of the vessel is pointing north 45 degrees east, sir."

"That we have heard and the stern is pointing exactly the other way. What else are you trying to establish, Mr Haight?"

"Sir, north 45 degrees east is practically the angle at which we say she was heading when she hit us and not southeast as Captain Kendall has claimed. The position of the vessel on the bottom supports our argument, sir."

Seventy-one

"I think the heading of the wreck could be important," Judge Routhier told Lord Mersey and Judge McLeod. They were having drinks at the bar of the *Château Frontenac* after two weeks of intense testimony.

"It would mean that the *Empress* changed course in the fog," he continued.

"I'm not sure I understand the importance of the diver's testimony," Lord Mersey said.

Judge McLeod seemed unconvinced.

"The *Empress* was hit amidships," McLeod said, "and then for 14 minutes, the liner drifted on the current before sinking. Its bearing could easily have changed."

Routhier decided to argue the point.

"I don't think a ship that is 180 yards long and weighs over 14,000 tons is going to change direction very much drifting on the current. Remember that we have water pouring into the engine-room and the ship is listing badly to starboard. The engines are stopped, and she's taking on water. This is not the case of a cork floating on a puddle of water."

"A puddle of water?" Lord Mersey laughed.

"I think our friend Routhier here is showing us his schoolboy knowledge of science," McLeod said with a laugh.

"Maybe my learned colleague never learned any science in school," Routhier said with a large dose of cynicism.

McLeod glared at Routhier but remained silent.

"Let's reserve judgment, gentlemen," Lord Mersey said, surprised by the sudden animosity between his colleagues. "We still have to hear the closing arguments."

McLeod had a chip on his shoulder and it was starting to weigh on his Quebec colleague who, having consumed two whiskies already and was working on a third, was not in the mood to duck a slight of any kind.

"Maybe my learned colleague never learned anything about ethics, preserving judicial impartiality and..."

"Gentlemen, please," Lord Mersey exhorted his colleagues.

"And avoiding conflicts of interest," Routhier continued. "Your meeting with the president of the CPR is reprehensible, to say the least."

"What's he talking about?" Lord Mersey turned to McLeod.

McLeod was red-faced and stunned by Routhier's words. He knew that nothing justified meeting privately with either party involved in the inquiry. It could get him kicked off the bench and provoke a huge scandal.

"I ran into Shea at the *Château Frontenac* one evening, sir. It was a mistake, but it will have no effect on my judgment."

"You should have told me," Lord Mersey said. "What did the man want?"

"Nothing, sir," McLeod said. "It was a social visit. We didn't talk about the inquiry. I made that clear. He talked about the sale of the *Storstad*, the business of running the CPR and the future of the company."

Routhier raised an eyebrow at this, but remained silent.

"Do you know the man," Lord Mersey asked.

"Of course I do, sir. I cannot deny it. I've met him in my role as Chief Justice of New Brunswick. We cross paths in Halifax and Montreal from time to time. It's inevitable in a small country like ours."

"Look, McLeod, I'm going to take you at your word," Lord Mersey said with growing indignation, "and at the same time hold you to a promise to avoid all contact with this man or any other party with an interest in the inquiry until we have completed our investigation."

"Yes, sir, I understand."

"If I hear anything to the contrary, I'll have you kicked off the inquiry and I'll make such a fuss that you will never work in any legal capacity again."

McLeod looked shaken.

The children's faces were horrible masks of death, many almost beyond recognition. Inside the temporary morgue, Inspector Mainguy stopped near a young boy whose face was better preserved. Clutching handkerchiefs to their noses, Alice and James stared at the boy's freckled face in stunned silence.

"These are the new ones. They were brought in after the divers went down," the Inspector said.

The new arrivals were laid out in their caskets on tables near the door in the hope that someone would claim them. Incense was burning, but the odour of decomposing flesh was suffocating.

"I'll leave you for a few moments. Take your time," the Inspector said to Alice.

He left to talk to the constable near the door as Alice and James went from table to table. Alice stood for a moment in front of a young boy whose face was disfigured and torso lacerated by multiple wounds. He had clearly been a handsome child in life, but in death, he was hideously mutilated. Alice felt compelled to examine the boy more closely. She examined the ruined face and slid her hands down the lifeless arms of the boy, discovering his identifying marks. A mole on an arm, a scar on a leg.

"It's him," she whispered to James. "I can't believe it. I've found my Jamie."

James looked at Alice dubiously. He asked himself whether she could recognize her son in the disfigured face or was she simply fantasizing.

"Are you sure, Alice?" he asked. "You have to be sure."

"He has the same round face and freckles. He has a birthmark on his arm. His hands are just like Tom's. This is my Jamie. This is my son. There can be no mistake."

James put his arm around Alice as she broke down and wept. Had her child suffered in the final moments or had death come quickly? Alice would never know.

Inspector Mainguy returned with the constable.

"Is this your boy, Mrs Bingham?"

"Yes, Inspector. This is my Jamie."

"A lot of the injuries are post-mortem, madam. They were in the water for quite some time."

"Thank you, Inspector," Alice sobbed. "You are very kind."

"*C'est notre devoir, madame.* When you're ready, give your details to the constable here and he'll have the body moved to the examination room where you will sign the register."

Alice nodded at the inspector.

Seventy-two

June 26, 1914

On a Friday morning, Butler Aspinall gave his final address to the court. The room was packed with journalists from around the world. Captain Andersen and John Griffin sat in a row behind Captain Kendall and Superintendent Walters. Haight sat at a table near the crown counsel Newcombe.

"I wish to say at the outset that our original statement concerning the collision has in its main features been established by the evidence," Aspinall said, "and by the admissions that have been made by the crew of the *Storstad* from day to day during the progress of this inquiry. We claimed that this collision was caused by the alteration of course by one or other of the ships and we said that what caused this collision was a porting and a hard-a-porting of the helm by the other vessel."

"It is remarkable, therefore, that it is now established beyond all doubt that the helm of the *Storstad* was ported and was hard-a-ported and, singularly enough, without any orders to that effect being given by the navigating officer of the *Storstad*. In addition, the evidence points inevitably to the conclusion that the *Storstad* had steerage way on her when the helm was put hard-a-port."

Aspinall drank from a glass of water on the podium and looked at the crowd.

"My Lords, I submit that this particular feature of the case - the hard-a-porting of the *Storstad* - is of immense value to the tribunal in determining where the truth of the story lies. Now if neither ship had altered course, we have shown that these two vessels would have passed one another safely, starboard to starboard passage - a left-hand passage - at a distance of half a mile. As we know, Captain Kendall altered his course to north 73 degrees east magnetic to bring him closer to the *Storstad*. Now if you have an object one point on your bow - assuming a fixed object - at a mile away, and you proceed on your course, you will pass that object at a distance of 1200 feet or 370 metres."

"In the case of a red to red passage - a right-hand passage - which is the position of the *Storstad* claim, Mr Saxe declared that when the fog shut us out, we were 2-3 miles distant and about a point on their port bow. Well then again, if the *Storstad* claim is right with the ships approaching red-to-red, I frankly admit it would bring about a perfectly safe lateral distance between the two ships as they passed."

"So the outcome of this evidence leads to the conclusion that whether we be green-to-green or red-to-red, there was no risk in passing at the lateral distance at which they were passing."

At his table, Haight was scribbling notes from Aspinall's address as Lord Mersey and his colleagues watched the crowd impassively.

"Another point," Aspinall continued, "is that we claimed we had lost our way, that we were, so to speak, a log upon the water, without steerage-way, and that we never did starboard our helm. We said that we blew three short blasts. Again, it is remarkable that the *Storstad* crew admitted that they heard us twice blow three short blasts."

"My Lords, one other feature of the case is that in order for the *Storstad* succeed against us, she will have to ask your Lordships to come to the conclusion that the cause of the collision was not the porting of the *Storstad*, but the starboarding of the *Empress*. Now, as I pointed out, she admits that she ported, she admits that she hard-a-ported, and she admits that the hard-a-porting was done without the orders of the navigating officer. She says that she did not alter course and I think I shall be able to demonstrate shortly that this cannot be the case."

Aspinall looked across at Captain Andersen and John Griffin in the audience.

"Now, for the *Storstad* to succeed against us, your Lordships will have to come to the conclusion that the testimony of Captain Kendall is a deliberate lie and a bad lie. It is perjury because it is a matter about which there can be no mistake. Whether he used his helm at all or whether he put it to starboard is the simplest question of fact that one can conceive. The Norwegians admit porting and hard-a-porting and say that it had no effect. So if Captain Kendall starboarded his vessel, then his testimony must be false, and we are speaking of the testimony of a man who has looked death in the face under very distressing circumstances, a man who has lost his ship, his shipmates and a very large number of his passengers."

"I submit, your Lordships, that you will be reticent to come to the conclusion that the testimony of this man was a deliberate lie."

Aspinall returned to his seat in the silent courtroom.

In the examination room of the temporary morgue, Alice held a handkerchief to her nose as she sat alone with her dead son Jamie and husband Tom. She had discovered her husband's body among the new arrivals soon after finding Jamie's. The two bodies were laid out on the tables. Tom's was relatively well preserved while her son's body had suffered a terrible beating.

James appeared with the constable.

"Alice, the constable needs you to sign the register for Tom's body, then we need to find a funeral home."

"Over here, Mrs Bingham," the constable said.

Alice stood up and followed the constable to the table. She picked up the pen, dipped the nib in the inkwell and signed her name in the register.

James helped her to stand up.

"It's going to be all right, Alice. You've found them. That's the important thing. They'll be buried together."

Alice nodded at James, and they left the room.

Seventy-three

June 27, 1914

On a Saturday, Charles Haight appeared before the court and gave his final address. The room was packed with people. Captain Andersen and John Griffin were again present, sitting behind Superintendent Walters for the CPR. Aspinall sat at a table with Newcombe.

"During the past ten days of this investigation, we have all been conscious of the fact that we are investigating a great tragedy," Haight said, "probably the worst tragedy that has been known in the shipping world. A clear night, on the wide waters of the St. Lawrence, with the lights all visible, absolutely no obstruction, and only two vessels in view. The course of each vessel is known, the position of each vessel is known, and the courses and positions are ones of absolute safety. Suddenly a curtain of fog is drawn and in fifteen minutes the *Empress of Ireland* has disappeared below the surface of the waters and over a thousand souls have gone down with her."

Haight paused and looked around the courtroom.

"The entire world wants to know why. Norway, I think, more insistently than anyone else wants to know how this happened and who was at fault. Before the St. Lawrence was even a name, Norway was proud of her ships and her sailors.

"I conceive, my Lords, that there is but one point in this case. Both sides admit that the vessels were on safe passing courses and that the position of each vessel was known. The question is therefore which ship changed her course? All the other questions sink into absolute unimportance."

Haight took on a grave demeanour.

"It is not pleasant to discuss the truth or falsity of testimony before this court. I would far rather argue that one side or the other was mistaken and not deliberately misstating facts, but I can see no way in which this Court can escape from the conclusion that what was done on one ship or the other, namely the change in course, was known when it was done. No ship would inadvertently change its heading by seven points as claimed by my revered colleague. There are compasses and in a fog, the compasses are watched and the crew of a ship that changed her course from north 76 degrees east to north by east, or a ship that changed her course from west by south seven points, some 78 degrees heading north 300 degrees west, knew that she had made the change in course. So clearly the witnesses from the vessel that changed course have deliberately falsified their testimony before this court."

Lord Mersey looked stunned by this statement, as did the other judges. Haight let the shocked silence hang in the air of the packed courtroom.

"Why would the *Empress* change course?" Haight asked. "This was asked of Captain Andersen. Why, if she was in a position of absolute safety, should she throw herself across the bow of the *Storstad*? To the witnesses of the *Empress*, the same question was put. Why would the *Storstad* have changed her course seven points, when she was on her way to Father Point, and then run straight to the North Shore? The only possible explanation is that one of the ships lost control and made a change of course."

"The testimonies of Galt, his fellow officers, the pilot of the *Alden*, and even that of Murphy, indicated that the steering mechanism of the *Empress* was not working properly. Evidence, given by others including the architects, supports the idea that the steering could have been a problem the night of the accident. This would also explain the very curious behaviour of Captain Kendall in suddenly putting his engines from full speed ahead to full speed astern - even at the risk of wrecking them - and stopping his vessel in less than two minutes."

"On the contrary, Mr Aspinall bases his entire case on the proposition that we could steer, that our ship navigated well, that she did steer and indeed that she has such great facility in steering that with her wheel a-port one minute after she had been slowed for two minutes and stopped for three or four minutes, she ran a mile against the current and changed her heading seven points. Our steering qualities are not only admitted, but are made the basis of the argument by the other side."

Haight paused for a long moment to drink from a glass of water and to gauge the effect of his argument. There was a sudden buzz of whispered conversation in the courtroom.

"I will have quiet here," Lord Mersey growled, rapping his gavel on the table. "Mr Haight, you will continue."

"My learned friend," Haight said, "has invited your Lordships to find that parts of my story are not true. I say that I defy my learned friend to find one man who knows anything about navigation who will believe that Captain Kendall put his engines full speed astern when the lights of the *Storstad* could still be seen and when he knew they were on a course that meant a clearance of half a mile to two miles. It is perfectly inconceivable that any man would risk the wrecking of his entire engine-room by ordering such a manoeuvre."

"I submit to your Lordships that there is a good deal of testimony to substantiate my theory that the steering gear broke down. The orders that Captain Kendall gave, the things that he did when the *Empress* first sighted the *Storstad* before entering the fog, seem to indicate not that an emergency was confronting the cool, efficient British Master, but that the Master had for some reason lost his balance. The whole testimony of what he did is feverish. It is absolutely different from what you would expect to find with reference to a man who, in a crisis, must act with a cool head."

"We have the evidence that due to the design of the stern, the rudders of the *Empress of Ireland* and the *Empress of Britain* were changed to improve the ship's steering capacity. We have the direct evidence of the men of the Alden and the pilot Lapierre, who only three or four hours before this tragedy occurred, testified that the *Empress* crowded them clear up on the North shore after zigzagging back and forth shutting red and green lights out four or five times."

Haight looked briefly at his notes.

"Your Lordships will, I am sure, agree with me that the witness Galt was unquestionably called out of order. I knew when he was called that his testimony had in advance been discredited. I realized that it would be considered the testimony of a man who had come to me with evidence to sell and who could be had at a price. But as your Lordships look back at the incident, has it not changed a little in perspective? Boys of lowly birth..."

"What?" Lord Mersey interrupted, with a hand on his ear.

"Boys of lowly birth," Haight repeated in a louder voice,

"have in times past done brave things and English boys are among the number. Mr Galt certainly had some courage. If he wanted to sell his testimony, he soon learned that no pieces of silver were forthcoming. He submitted himself to a cross-examination that would have tested any man."

"If the testimony of Galt is found to be true and that of the men of the Alden and the pilot Lapierre, they provide a reason for this accident and explain why the *Empress* changed her course. I submit to your Lordships that the *Empress* blew a running whistle when she entered the fog, as any reasonable ship would do. Several witnesses came forward to testify that they had heard a long blast from the *Empress* and this whistle was not only blown once, but was repeated. The *Empress* entered the fog at a speed of 17 knots and the three whistles came several minutes after the fog shut both vessels out from view."

"I think the evidence shows clearly that the *Empress* was moving ahead at the time of the collision. The testimony of the naval architect Hillhouse strongly supported this idea. The *Storstad* came out of the wound and swung around one hundred degrees before disappearing astern. The only satisfactory explanation for this swing is the forward movement of the *Empress*."

Haight paused, looking up at the judges.

"I submit to your Lordships that the *Storstad* was maintaining a course west by south. This means that the *Empress* at the moment of the collision was on a course crossing our path of north 39 degrees east and today she lies on the bottom pointing exactly north 45 degrees east."

"That is the diver's evidence?" asked Lord Mersey.

"Yes, my Lord."

A ponderous silence followed. Haight let the silence stretch out for a good minute before he spoke again.

"Mr Aspinall argued yesterday that Captain Kendall must be believed because he had recently faced death, had lost his ship and had been connected with a disaster, which meant the loss of over a thousand lives. Now, must he be believed for those reasons? Is it not more likely that because he lost his ship and a thousand lives, he would not dare face the world with a frank admission that he had been at fault?"

The courtroom broke out in whispered conversation. This time, Lord Mersey let the voices die down of their own accord. Haight waited until he had the rapt attention of everyone before speaking.

"I submit, my Lords, that the heading of the wreck on the bottom was the heading of the *Empress* at the time of the collision and that because of that heading, the *Empress* alone is to blame."

Seventy-four

June 29, 1914

Captain Kendall wondered what to make of the summons. He had collected the card in his box at the front desk of the *Château Frontenac*. He was to go to a meeting at the CPR offices that same afternoon. He had been on half-pay for the length of the inquiry. Was this the last straw? Was he to be sacked or sent out to some remote outpost of the CPR empire? Hong Kong, Sydney or maybe Auckland.

As he entered the conference room, he was surprised by the warm reception. Sir Thomas Shea, the president of CPR operations, was all smiles as he shook his hand and patted him on the back. Superintendent Walters, who stood nearby, couldn't hide his disapproval and barely managed a nod in his direction.

"Well done, Captain," Shea said.

"Thank you, sir, but I see no reason to rejoice."

"I can see that you're a terrible pessimist. Cheer up, old chap. The CPR is a big company. We have a bright future ahead of us. Nobody will let us go belly up because of the loss of one ship. Haven't you seen the papers?"

Kendall shook his head.

"Archduke Franz Ferdinand, the heir to the Austrian

throne, was assassinated yesterday. They say the Austrians are furious and are going to declare war on Serbia and their allies, the Russians. War is coming and you know what that means."

Kendall stared blankly at Shea and Walters.

"My dear fellow, it means that nobody will remember the *Empress of Ireland* in a very short time. The world will have moved on."

Kendall attempted to grasp the significance of Shea's words.

"Take it from me, a war is coming between the great powers. This means that you'll be back in command again before you know it," Shea concluded, nodding at Walters.

"You've got a fortnight's leave at the expense of the company," Walters said, grudgingly handing Kendall his boarding pass and instructions.

"Mr Shea's decision, not mine," he added.

Kendall turned to Shea.

"Well, thank you, sir."

Shea nodded his approval before he dismissed the captain. Kendall looked at the two men and left the room.

A stage had been set up to receive the purser's safe in the lobby of the Bank of Montreal on *rue St-Pierre* in the old city. A locksmith had been busy for hours drilling holes in the door of the safe, which was as large as a telephone booth. It had been removed from the *Empress* by the divers of the salvage company after blowing a hole in the side of the vessel.

The salvage team had first removed some 318 mailbags from the ship containing letters, parcels, and registered documents. The value of the money orders alone added up to over $90,000. The divers had then removed the silver bullion from the ship, all 212 bars with a value of over $1 million.

Then came the recovery of the safe, which was a huge undertaking. The divers had to unbolt the safe from the bulkhead and, using steel cables, pull it down a passageway in the sunken wreck to a hole in the side. It was then hauled to the surface and brought to Quebec City for the opening ceremony.

The purser's safe contained an unknown quantity of passenger valuables, and the CPR was liable for any losses. The company had insisted that the safe remain unopened and undamaged during the salvage operation, so that no claimant could say their valuables had been lost or replaced with cheap imitations. The liability claims for lost valuables against the White Star line, owners of the *Titanic,* were still ongoing in the courts after two years and the claims amounted to well over twice the cost of the ship. So the CPR and their insurers were dead set on avoiding the same predicament, whatever the cost.

It was a Saturday morning and a large crowd of bankers, lawyers, company officials, relatives of the deceased and reporters gathered in the lobby of the bank. The salvage company boss, William Stobo, stood next to Thomas Shea of the CPR and bank manager Arthur Nash, waiting for the dramatic moment when all would be revealed.

The cameras were ready and primed. The locksmith had drilled the last hole and was brushing away the metal shavings, when an assistant photographer accidentally set off a pan of flash powder, a potent mixture of magnesium and potassium chlorate, dazzling the attendance and sending people into coughing fits.

The locksmith put down the drill and grabbed the door handle. He pulled, disengaging the interior latches, and a murmur went through the crowd as a solid metal click was heard. The crowd leaned forward, jockeying for position, as the locksmith received a nod from the bank manager. He then gave a hard pull and the door swung open.

The crowd was again stunned by the bright light of the flash and the sight of the empty safe. There was nothing to see but a few canvas bags and a row of locked compartments. It seemed to be a very poor return for such a valiant recovery effort. The crowd had expected the safe to be packed with cash and jewellery based on the claims made by the passengers.

A sigh of disappointment went up from the crowd and the people started to collect themselves, departing the room. Shea turned to the bank manager.

"Well, that was a bit of a letdown. I was expecting many more bags of valuables."

"I think we'll find quite a few things in that safe," Nash advised, "though not as much as the press expected."

"I'm sure you're right, sir."

After the accountants had added it all up, the sum total of the valuables in cash, cheques, and negotiable paper in the purser's safe came to no more than half a percent of the amount claimed as lost by the passengers and their families. The liability cases against the CPR and the insurers soon became scarce, as embarrassed claimants withdrew their lawsuits.

On a sandy beach on the *Ile d'Orléans,* Alice and Vicky sat on a blanket, under a parasol, enjoying a picnic. Vicky stood up and went over to help young René, who was busy frying fish in a pan over a small fire.

Nearby, Kendall and Galt, in shirtsleeves and rolled-up pants, walked in the shallow water. A small dinghy was pulled up on the shore and a schooner was anchored in deep water a short distance away.

"You're leaving us tomorrow?" Galt asked the captain.

"Yes. It will be good to get home," Kendall said. "What about yourself?"

"I'll stay a week or two and give Alice a hand."

"Wasn't she to return to Toronto?"

"She's staying on here for the funeral and may find work with Pauline's help. She's a schoolteacher, so I'm sure she'll find something."

"You're taking quite an interest in the girl."

Galt winked at the captain.

"What will you do when you get home, Henry?"

"I have two weeks off and then I'm going to have to start looking for another job with the company."

"Your days as a captain are over?"

"I would think so. I doubt they'll be hiring me again in that capacity."

Seventy-five

It had been a long day for Alice. She had been to the funeral service for her husband and child, buried together in the Mount Hermon Cemetery. Vicky, Pauline, and James had accompanied her.

Vicky was full of questions about dead people, and why her parents' bodies had never been found. She stood next to Alice at the gravesite and cried when Alice was overcome by emotion during the ceremony. In many ways, she was burying her own parents alongside Tom and Jamie and wishing them well in their next life. She fell asleep in the calèche on their return from the cemetery.

Alice put Vicky to bed early. The child was exhausted and asked Alice to tuck her in and kiss her good night. After a light supper, James sat with Alice on the couch in Mrs Pelletier's parlour, after Pauline had gone up to bed.

"Vicky is a sweet kid. She's obviously taken with you, Alice."

"Yes, she is. It was like having a daughter with me at the cemetery."

"She's a lovely child."

"I never imagined having a girl after Jamie. It's so different with a girl."

"You'll have to return her to her uncle eventually, Alice.

He's next of kin. It might be better to do it sooner rather than later."

"You know, I have had some time to think about things these last few days. I've made up my mind. I am going to adopt Vicky. She needs a mother, and she helps keep my mind off Tom and Jamie."

"You're not serious, Alice, are you?"

"Yes, I am. Vicky needs a mother and I love her."

"I agree that she's everything one could want in a daughter, but you need to be sure."

"I am sure, James."

"You'll have to take this up with the uncle. Is he married?"

"No, he's not," Alice said with a mischievous air. "I think Vicky and I will visit Donald on his farm, during the harvest when he's busiest."

James laughed.

"I think only a woman could think of something like that," he said, teasing Alice, who jabbed him with an elbow.

"A farmer with a crop to get in," Alice said, "won't have any time for a small child."

Seventy-six

July 11, 1914

Two weeks later, Lord Mersey and his colleagues made their report. The inquiry had been a fact-finding tribunal. It was not a criminal nor a civil procedure, so the conclusions were not binding. The courtroom was crowded and stifling hot. Many of the reporters were fanning themselves with their hats. Captain Andersen sat with John Griffin, while Haight and Aspinall sat at their respective tables near Newcombe. The room quieted as Lord Mersey started to read the conclusion to his report.

"The stories of the two captains are irreconcilable and who is to blame depends on whose story you believe. The main issue for us was to decide whether the ships were expected to pass red-to-red or green-to-green."

In the Empress wheelhouse, Quartermaster Murphy was at the helm and First Officer Johnson was giving an order by the telegraph to the engine-room. Third Officer Moore, Second Quartermaster Sharples and a boy were standing by. Captain Kendall entered from the chartroom and gave Johnson the heading.

"Port the helm, Johnson, north by 76 degrees east. I'm going up to check the (magnetic) compass."

"Yes, sir. North 76 degrees east, Mr Moore."

Kendall climbed the ladder to the upper bridge. Johnson watched him go and then left the wheelhouse.

The fog had come up quickly. On the Storstad, Toftenes saw the Empress' green light change to red and the masthead lights start to separate. After a moment, the Empress' red light disappeared completely in the fog. Toftenes ordered Saxe to keep on course.

A furious Captain Kendall bolted from the upper bridge of the Empress and hurried down the ladder to the wheelhouse.

"Moore, you're off course!" he barked. *"We're showing red."*

Moore and Murphy checked the compass, which was now showing north 87 degrees east, a full point off course.

"Bring the helm to starboard, two points."

"Yes, sir," Moore said.

"Where's Johnson?"

"Sorry, sir," Moore stammered. *"I haven't seen him."*

Quartermaster Murphy brought the wheel over, as Moore blew a long blast on the ship's whistle.

"We have come to the conclusion," Lord Mersey told the courtroom, "that the first officer of the *Storstad*, Toftenes, was mistaken if he thought that the *Empress* had any intention of passing red-to-red (right-hand). This mistake would have been of no consequence if both ships had kept on course. The question as to who was to blame resolved itself into a simple issue of deciding which of the ships changed her course in the fog."

"I have had men sacked for less," Kendall yelled angrily at Johnson as he returned to the wheelhouse. "No officer leaves his post without permission on this ship! Is that perfectly clear?"

"Yes, sir."

"Never, do that again, Johnson."

A long blast was heard from the Storstad.

Kendall returned his attention to the thickening fog, knowing all too well that Johnson was taking advantage of their friendship. He watched the quartermaster struggling with the wheel as the ship sheered, ending up on a course of north 45 degrees east.

Moore checked the navigation compass.

"You've gone over too far over, Murphy, bring her back a bit."

"Give me a minute, sir. I'll get it right."

"We're in the fog now. It won't make any difference. Keep on course," Kendall said. "We may be able to get clear of the fog."

"Yes, sir."

"The captain's decision to put his engines full speed astern and to stop his vessel is proof of his uneasiness," Lord Mersey said, "and a consciousness that his ship was possibly in too close proximity to the *Storstad*, but cannot be considered as an unseamanlike act nor can it be considered as a cause of the accident."

On the bridge of the Empress, Kendall looked over the side to see whether his vessel had stopped. Suddenly, out of the fog, appeared the red and green lights of the Storstad bearing down on him. Time was suspended.

"Johnson, full speed ahead," Kendall bellowed.

"Full speed ahead it is, sir."

As Kendall grabbed the megaphone, Johnson called down to the engine-room. Kendall waved his arms in a futile attempt to stop the Storstad. As the Empress men watched in horror, the Storstad slammed into the liner. They hardly felt the impact, but could clearly hear the grating sound of collapsing metal plates.

"There is no ground for saying that the course of the *Empress of Ireland* was ever changed in the sense that the wheel was wilfully moved," Lord Mersey said, "but as the hearing proceeded another explanation was propounded, namely that the vessel changed her course due to some uncontrollable movement of the wheel which was based on the hypothesis that the steering gear was out of order and the ship steered badly. The principal witness on the point as to the steering gear was a man named Galt, a quartermaster on the *Empress*. We are of the opinion that this witness gave his evidence badly and made so unsatisfactory a witness that we cannot rely on his testimony."

"In the case of the men of the *Alden*, they did not speak of any behaviour of the vessel which would suggest jamming, and it is to be observed that the allegations that the vessel sheered from side to side on this occasion are entirely different from the allegations of Galt that the wheel jammed. On the whole question of the steering gear and rudder, we are of the opinion that the allegations as to their conditions are not well founded. We have consulted our advisors and they concur in this opinion."

The floor of the wheelhouse was canted at a crazy angle as the men on the bridge struggled to maintain their posts. Kendall called the engine-room.

"Give me all you can! I'll try to beach her."

Johnson looked at the smokestacks.

"There is no more steam, Captain," Johnson said.

"Johnson, blow the siren," Kendall ordered. "Prepare to abandon ship."

Johnson stared at him, shocked by the finality of the order.

"Get to it, man!"

"Yes, sir."

Kendall turned to Moore, who, like Johnson, seemed frozen to the spot. He could read the fear on the man's weathered face.

"Moore, get an SOS off on the Marconi. Hurry, the ship is sinking. Position twenty miles east of Rimouski. Got that?"

Moore nodded and left for the radio room.

"We regret to have to impute blame to anyone in connection with this lamentable disaster," Lord Mersey concluded, "and we would not do so if we felt that any reasonable alternative was left to us. We can, however, come to no other conclusion than that, Mr Toftenes was wrong and negligent in altering his course in the fog, as he undoubtedly did, and that he was wrong and negligent in keeping the navigation of the vessel in his own hands and in failing to call the captain when he saw the fog coming in."

"Such is the conclusion at which we have arrived on the question as to who is to blame for the disaster. But a question of much greater public interest and importance remains to be considered: why the ship sank so quickly and what steps, if any, can be taken to prevent the terrible consequences which so often follow from such disasters..."

"This is a lie," Captain Andersen roared, standing up and shaking his fist at the judges. "They are telling lies."

His outburst set off pandemonium in the crowd, with reporters trying to get closer to hear what Andersen had to say. Amid the clamour, Haight shouldered his way over to Andersen.

"Sit down, Captain," Haight said, putting a hand on his arm.

"Tell him, Mr Haight," Andersen said. "This is not so."

Newspaper reporters rushed out of the courtroom to file their reports.

"Order in the court. Bailiff, we need order in the court," Lord Mersey shouted above the tumult.

"This is a lie. This is totally unfair," Andersen yelled. "This Lord Mersey. What he think? We are foreigners, so we are lying all the time."

"Order in the court, order in the court," the bailiff said in a loud voice.

"He believe nothing we say, this man," Andersen shouted. "We do not wear the gold, the gold braid and the buttons, but we are damned good sailors."

Lord Mersey and the judges stood up, waiting for the chaos to subside.

"Mr. Haight. What is your opinion?" a journalist asked.

"I have nothing to say except that we were badly treated," Haight said. "I think our evidence was ignored."

"There is a word for this, Mr Haight," Andersen said in a loud voice. "It is 'scapegoat'. Someone must pay, so we Norwegians make good scapegoats. Yes?"

Andersen raised his fist again in defiance and was led out of the courtroom by John Griffin.

Seventy-seven

Alice and Vicky sat next to James as he drove a two-wheeled, pony trap down a dirt track towards a farm in rural Ontario. The house was an old sharecropper's shack with bare wooden walls and a tin roof. Behind the house, there was a barn and a cornfield where a farmer was going from row to row with a handbasket.

When he noticed the buggy, the man stopped what he was doing and shaded his eyes with one hand, trying to see who was coming to visit. The driver of the buggy was a well-dressed young man wearing a Panama hat sitting next to a woman and a child in summer dresses. It couldn't be his neighbours. No one had time to visit friends during the hectic harvest season.

Uncle Donald put down the handbasket and started towards the house. He would have to shoo them away right quick, with all the work he had to do before nightfall.

On the porch, Uncle Donald, unshaven in a sweat-stained shirt and dirty overalls, poured tea into china cups on a wooden milk crate opposite Alice and Vicky sitting on an old couch. He sat on a stool near James in an old rocking chair.

"I've come a long way to see you," Alice said. "I thought it was time for a visit."

"Yes, ma'am, it's good to see you and young Vicky again."

Vicky sat close to Alice, holding her hand.

"I have taken good care of your niece, sir."

"I can see that with my own eyes, miss. She looks fine."

"She's a remarkable girl."

"She looks a lot like her mother. My sister had the same blonde hair."

Donald drank his tea and then pushed a biscuit across the milk crate in Vicky's direction, but she ignored it. James watched Alice with growing concern. She seemed hesitant to come to the point of the visit.

"I want to look after Vicky, sir."

"You mean like a governess? I doubt I can put you up. I don't have any room here, miss."

"No, not like a governess."

"I hardly have room for Vicky."

"Yes, I can see that."

"I ain't got no experience raisin' children, miss."

"I care for Vicky, sir."

"I can see that she likes you."

Vicky cuddled close to Alice.

"Miss Vicky will have to earn her keep here," Donald said. "She'll have to haul water, feed the animals and work around the farm. There's a school, but it's a long hike. I don't know whether they'll take her."

"I see," Alice said.

"She'll have to learn to cook."

"Yes, of course."

"Butcher chickens, sweep out the stable, and weed the garden. There's a lot of work around a farm, you know. Do you think she's ready for it?"

By now, Vicky was clinging fearfully to Alice, her eyes welling up with tears. James had watched the conversation with growing frustration, as if it were a tennis match that neither adversary wanted to lose. He could stand it no longer.

"For God's sake, Alice, tell the man what you want."

"I want to adopt Vicky, sir," she blurted. "I want to raise her as my own."

James gave a sigh of relief.

"You want to adopt my niece?" Donald asked, incredulous.

"Yes, I do."

"Well, I never. I thought you wanted to dump her on me. That's why I was telling you about all the hard work."

Donald turned his attention to Vicky.

"What do you say, Vicky?"

"I love Alice. She's my mummy now."

"Well, I never."

James pulled out two copies of the adoption papers from a leather briefcase. He put them on the milk crate in front of Donald.

"These are the adoption papers," James said, "to make it official. I had them prepared by a lawyer."

"Sure, I have no objection. I think Vicky would be better off with you, Miss Alice, but I have one condition."

Alice looked nervously at James.

"I need to do the right thing by my sister," Donald said. "She was a good, God-fearing woman. She would have wanted it. It would be real important for her."

"I'm sure she would, sir."

"Does Vicky know her alphabet?"

Vicky jumped up to recite the alphabet.

"A, B, C, D..."

"Can she write real good?"

"I can write real...very well, sir."

"Good, 'cause your mum is in heaven and she's lookin' down on us right now."

Vicky looked up at the rafters and the walls of the shack covered with faded yellow newsprint. She was disappointed to not see her mother in the dusty rays of light beaming off the walls.

"Your mum was a good Christian woman, Vicky. She went to church every Sunday."

Alice put her arm around Vicky and waited.

"My only condition, Miss Alice, is that Vicky write to me at least once a year to tell me how she's doin', where she's livin', where she's goin' to school and to church. Her mum will want to know those things. She'll want me to watch out for her."

"Vicky can do it," Alice exclaimed, beside herself with joy. "Can't you Vicky?"

Vicky nodded and embraced Alice. Donald picked up the adoption papers in his rough hands and turned to look at the last page.

"If you can put that in your paper, young man, I'll agree to allow Miss Alice to adopt Vicky."

"Of course," James said.

Vicky glanced at Alice, not quite comprehending what had just happened. She looked forward to writing to Uncle Donald. She would use an ink pen and make beautiful letters, just as the teacher had taught her at school.

Seventy-eight

September 8, 1939

It was not yet noon on a sunny day in London as Captain Kendall, now retired and well into his sixties, sat on a bench watching the Thames River from the embankment. In the distance, he noticed a man approaching. He was wearing a dark suit and a fedora, and his hair was going grey near the temples. Over the years, James Galt - the gum-chewing sailor - had become an insurance salesman for Lloyds of London.

"Henry, how are you?" Galt said to his old friend.

"Fine, but a little slower."

Kendall stood up to shake Galt's hand. Together, they walked along the path.

"When did you get in?" Galt asked.

"I arrived yesterday by train. You know the Germans torpedoed the *Athenia* last week."

"Yes, that's all the talk around the office. An unarmed passenger vessel. The director at Lloyds says the Germans are in violation of the Hague Convention. The attack was launched on the same day that we declared war on Germany."

"They were lucky that the ship remained afloat long enough to get the passengers off. They were rescued by passing cargo ships."

"I heard that the Germans are denying any responsibility," Galt said. "They say that we intentionally sank the ship, and that they had no U-boats in the area."

"Another terrible war is upon us," Kendall said. "How are Alice and the children?"

"They're fine. You know Vicky went out to Australia. Peter's at Cambridge."

"That's very good. He must be a bright lad."

"He is."

"Something quite remarkable has come up, old chap. I told you a long time ago that you had been an inspiration to me during that difficult period during the *Empress* inquiry. Well, it's true. You were quite the courageous young man. Not all of us were proud of what we had to do."

"Well, it was a very difficult time for you, Henry."

"Yes, it was. I got a letter from the American lawyer Haight several weeks ago. It's all the more surprising because he died last year."

Galt gave him a quizzical look.

"It appears that his son took over the firm after his death and found the letter in his father's things. The old man had written it two years ago and forgotten to post it. Funny how you forget things when you get older. Anyway, in this extraordinary letter, he told me that our friend Johnson had gone to see him with an offer to change his testimony."

Galt was dumbstruck.

"Change his testimony?"

"In his original testimony, he said that he hadn't seen the masthead lights of the *Storstad*. Later, he retracted and said he had seen them. He tried to do a deal with Shea and Walters, but when he wasn't called back by the inquiry, he must have gone over to the other side."

"That's incredible. I would never have thought."

"I had testified that the *Storstad* lights were open on the starboard side and they were showing green. I never actually saw their green light before they disappeared in the fog."

"But you were mistaken about the lights, weren't you, Henry?"

"Yes, I believe I was. The company line was that they were showing green, not red. If the *Storstad* had been showing its green light, its starboard side, then they would have been obliged to get out of our way under the rules of navigation, and not the contrary."

"So the *Empress* was on a crossing course?"

"Yes, that is the only credible explanation of the collision. I feared a collision; that's why I put our engines astern to stop the ship."

"What happened?"

"Haight was tempted to put Johnson back on the stand. The price was high, and the Norwegians were sorely tempted, but eventually they did nothing. They feared a scandal."

"My God, Johnson was going to do that?"

"Charles Haight was a brilliant attorney and very thorough, no doubt about it. You remember the detective?"

"You mean Walters' man? The one who was keeping an eye on you at the time?"

"Yes, but he didn't work for Walters, he worked for Haight. He was hired to keep an eye on Johnson, not me. They didn't trust Johnson. They thought he might be a plant to undermine their case."

Galt looked fondly at the older man.

"I remember it all so well," Kendall said. "The Norwegians got the blame and I returned to my old job within weeks. A month later, in August '14, I was commanding the *Montrose* again, with the *Montreal* in tow, running out of Antwerp before the Germans arrived. It was almost as if the *Empress* disaster had never happened, but I never forgot the shame I felt—the testimony I gave— and the loss of innocent lives. I still think about those last moments when the *Empress* went down."

AFTERWORD

The story of the *Empress* disaster is full of heart-wrenching tales. A thousand men, women and children drowned that night in the fog on the St. Lawrence River. Many of the passengers were first-generation Canadians on their way back to the old country for a visit. Their deaths provoked long periods of unhappiness and changed the course of their children's lives.

A woman was found walking naked on the shore near Rimouski on June 2, 1914. She was believed to be a foreign national, possibly from Sweden, and a passenger on the *Empress* according to David Zeni in his excellent book "Forgotten Empress". The newspapers at the time reported that she was walking in a "daze" and had been driven insane by the tragedy. I have unabashedly adapted this poor woman's story for my main character, Alice, who lost her husband and child in the collision. Alice managed to survive by floating on a wooden crate which was washed ashore.

The foreign woman was not alone. Among the bodies washed ashore, there was a young girl discovered by a local resident, thirteen-year-old Eileen Tuggy. Her people built a coffin for the girl and sent her body to Quebec City for identification. When the coffin was opened at Pier 27, a wreath of lilies was found resting on the body with a note from Eileen which read: "Kindly accept my kindest and sincerest sympathy. May she rest in peace. If identified, I would like to know."

After reading the novel, many of you will concur with me that the Mersey Inquiry was a whitewash. The judges laid the blame on the Norwegians and freed the CPR from any charges of wrongdoing and possible lawsuits. The judges didn't even blame Captain Kendall for not ordering the closing of the watertight doors and portholes before the ship entered the fog, which was company policy at the time. If the captain had done so, it might have delayed the sinking of the ship and permitted the crew to save more lives.

The testimony before the inquiry was often irreconcilable, in particular, the colour of the navigation lights. The *Storstad* crew told the inquiry that the *Empress* appeared on their port bow (red light or left side) and the passenger liner showed first its green light and then a red light before disappearing in the fog. The *Empress* crew maintained that the *Storstad* appeared on their starboard bow (green light or right side) and the collier was showing the masthead lights on its starboard side and a green light. Clearly, someone was mistaken or someone was lying.

If you look at the diagram (on page 100) of the relative position of the ships, you will see that from the *Storstad* point of view (see the lower portion of the diagram), there was never any risk of collision after the *Empress* had shown her red light as she entered the fog. It was going to be a red-to-red or right-hand passage. The *Storstad* had absolutely no reason to change course in the fog and, being the slower of the two ships at 10 knots against the tide, they had no chance to outrun a passenger liner like the *Empress* at 17 knots. All they had to do was to maintain the same heading and they would pass safely through the fog.

From the *Empress* version of events, the *Storstad* was showing a green light so the passenger liner had to be located on the other side of the *Storstad*'s course (see the top portion of the diagram). If both ships were showing their green lights, then it was going to be a green-to-green or left-hand passage with no danger of a collision.

Aspinall maintained in his closing argument that it really didn't matter if the *Empress* was showing a red or a green light, it would have been very unlikely they would have collided with the other ship if both vessels had remained on course. According to Saxe, when the fog came in, the *Empress* was 2-3 miles distant and about a point on their port bow. They would have passed each other in the fog by around 1200 feet or 370 metres if no one had changed course.

If we believe that the *Storstad* was truly showing its red light and the *Empress* was showing its green light, as they claimed at the inquiry, then the ships were on a crossing course and there was a real danger of collision. Of course, if the ships were showing red-to-red or green-to-green, to have a collision, one of the ships had to change their heading in the fog. Remember that the *Storstad* ran into the starboard side of the *Empress* at an angle of three points or 33 degrees, according to Captain Andersen's testimony.

It is my opinion that the *Empress* must have changed course in the fog by bringing the helm to starboard from north 76 degrees east to around north 45 degrees east, which put them on a crossing path with the other ship. This change was suggested by Haight in his closing argument.

Of course, if the *Empress* had not changed course, then the *Storstad* must have. The judges believed that the *Storstad* was hard-a-ported from west by south (258 degrees) bringing it across the path of the *Empress* to north 291 degrees west. That would mean that the Storstad changed course by around 33 degrees, which seems unlikely when they were so confident of their position. In Haight's closing argument, he talks about north 300 degrees west, so my figure is quite close.

The hard-a-porting Saxe mentioned was obviously a move to maintain their course when the *Storstad* was almost stopped in the water and trying to maintain its heading against a tidal current of 2.5 knots. The collier couldn't have travelled very far off course if it did, because it barely had steerage way, and there seems to be no justification for doing so. Why would the *Storstad* change its course so radically if they were convinced that they could safely pass the *Empress* red-to-red?

Furthermore, we must remember that the *Empress* was a very fast ship establishing records for transatlantic crossings and there was a good deal of evidence indicating that sheering was a problem for the ship in tight river estuaries like the St. Lawrence River or the River Mersey. Fast ships were a law unto themselves and they only observed the rules of navigation when it was in their interest.

With regard to political intervention in the inquiry, I believe that Robert Borden's government in Ottawa was beside itself worrying about the blame game going on in Quebec City. The CPR was a flagship company, a bit like GM or Bombardier in Canada or Boeing in the US today. The CPR had built the railroads and opened up the west. Their steamships carried new immigrants to settle the lands. They were the pride and joy of Canadian politicians and could do no wrong. So the Minister of Marine and Fisheries, John Douglas Hazen, who had ordered the inquiry in the first place, would have been very concerned about the outcome and under pressure to make it all go away. He hailed from New Brunswick like Chief Justice Ezekiel McLeod, so these men would certainly have communicated the concerns of the Borden government to Lord Mersey.

From the testimony at the inquiry, Lord Mersey appeared to be surprisingly ignorant of maritime affairs. His comments show his complete lack of understanding of navigational rules. He tended to bully the witnesses at the inquiry and his treatment of Galt (real name Galway) was appalling. I would not be surprised if he tired of such a difficult case and simply asked his colleagues to choose a guilty party.

It was politically expedient to blame the Norwegians. A small country which exercised little influence on the transatlantic crossings business dominated by British, French, American and German interests. The admission of hard-a-porting by the *Storstad* moments before the collision was all the judges needed to find a guilty party while they ignored the rest of the evidence.

An inquiry conducted later at the Norwegian Consulate General in Montreal ultimately exonerated the *Storstad* and Captain Andersen. The *Storstad* was seized for damages as requested by the Canadian Pacific Steamship company (the CPR) in a $2 million lawsuit against the A.F. Klaveness shipping line and later sold for a sum of $175,000. A total of $3 million worth of damages were filed: $2 million for the loss of the *Empress*, $600,000 for lost property and $469,000 for life insurance claims. The $175,000 was divided among the claimants.

In the weeks following the inquiry, Kendall was nominated marine superintendent in Antwerp. In August, he managed to save two Canadian Pacific ships, the *Montrose* and the *Montreal*, loaded with refugees from the hands of the invading

Germans. For most of the war years, he served on the Allen liner, the *Calgarian*, as second-in-command and was torpedoed off the coast of Northern Ireland and Scotland by a German submarine. He survived by sliding down a rope to a passing trawler.

Captain Thomas Andersen was reassigned to the *Storstad*, which had been repaired and resold to Norwegian interests. Andersen and his crew were torpedoed off the coast of Ireland in March 1917 but also managed to survive.

ACKNOWLEDGEMENTS

I would like to thank my wife Andrée Tousignant, son Thomas Kinsey, my editor Doug Sutherland and readers Clare Dyer and Carole Beauchamp, my daughters Eve and Josée Kinsey and everyone else who believed in this adventure and provided assistance. I would also like to thank my friend and collaborator Michel Pouliot, who did the early research on the story.

THE AUTHOR

Nicholas Kinsey is a Canadian / British writer and director of feature films and television dramas. He has been a successful director, scriptwriter, director of photography, film editor, and producer over a long career. He is the bestselling author of five historical novels and twenty feature and television drama screenplays. He is owner and producer at Cinegrafica Films since 2014 and writes a history blog. He lives in Quebec City, Canada.

His novels include:

Playing Rudolf Hess
An Absolute Secret
Shipwrecked Lives
Remembrance Man
White Slave: 15 Years a Barbary Slave

www.nicholaskinsey.com/
facebook @NicholasKinseyAuthor
twitter@KinseyAuthor

PLAYING RUDOLF HESS

One of the greatest mysteries of WWII

After parachuting into Scotland in 1941, the German Reichsminister Rudolf Hess is revealed to be an imposter. MI5 puts together a team of intelligence officers led by Paul Cummings and his German wife Claudia to investigate the Hess double. They are sent to Camp Z where Hess is being held in relative comfort following Churchill's orders. The team soon starts to uncover the imposter's secrets involving the shadowy Herr Oberst and his secret training by the SS. But the British government decides to bury the truth and it is only in 1973 that a British doctor confronts the imposter during a medical examination in Berlin and discovers the truth.

"Makes history come alive like a thriller"

"Must read, forgotten WWII story"

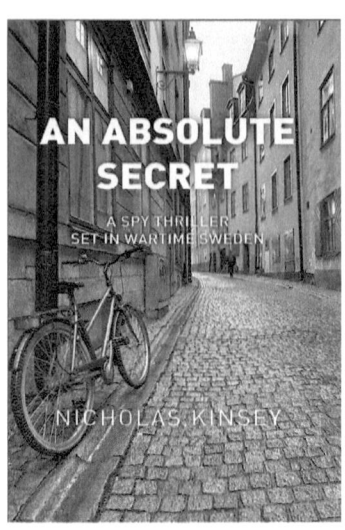

AN ABSOLUTE SECRET

A spy thriller based on real wartime intelligence operations in Sweden.

On his first assignment for MI6, British agent Peter Faye is sent to Stockholm to spy on German intelligence officer Karl-Heinz Kramer. At the British legation, he meets his new boss Bridget, a very proper, smart-as-a-whip, diplomat's daughter and immediately falls in love with her. They struggle to work together as they recruit an Austrian maid, Hanne, who works in the Kramer household. Hanne makes a copy of the key to Kramer's desk drawer and delivers secret documents to Peter and his driver Bernie who photograph them in a shed nearby. The documents are so sensitive they cause a huge commotion in London. With the help of a Swedish journalist, Peter discovers a network of Soviet moles working in British Intelligence and becomes the target of Soviet NKVD terror tactics.

"Kinsey has written a book that will comfortably sit along with the best writers of this genre. I thoroughly enjoyed this book and can wholeheartedly recommend." BookSirens

REMEMBRANCE MAN

Fear and despair during the 1832 cholera epidemic

During the 1832 cholera epidemic, Paolo works for his uncle as a gravedigger in Western Ontario. At night he earns a bonus from wealthy clients as a 'remembrance man' whose job is to watch over selected graves for signs of the undead. He discovers a young woman who has been buried alive and is drawn into a terrifying story of revenge and insanity. This is a tale of murder, greed and deceit, and the breakdown of society. Family members turn against family members, friends against friends, and soon everyone is out for themselves. Cholera victims are simply abandoned on the roads, and wagons are sent around to collect the bodies and bury them in cholera pits. During these dark days, stories spread about reopening coffins in which the dead had apparently revived after burial, only to die in a futile attempt to escape. No one wanted to bury a loved one who might still be alive, which led to the habit of keeping corpses around so that the families could be sure the person had really died.

> *"Rarely has a novelist managed to convey more vividly the breakdown of society during a cholera epidemic."*

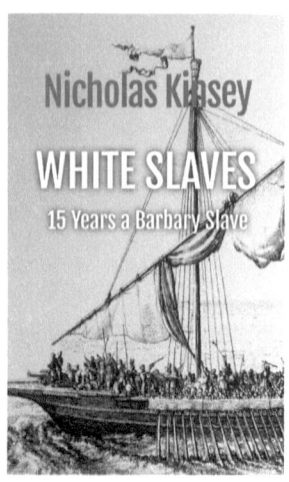

WHITE SLAVES: 15 YEARS A BARBARY SLAVE

The tragic story of the Baltimore captives

This brilliantly imagined novel tells the true story of the enslavement of the Baltimore captives and the horror of the Barbary slave trade. In the summer of 1631, the famous corsair and pirate Murad Reis attacked the peaceful fishing village of Baltimore, Ireland and seized 109 men, women and children subjecting them to a thirty-eight-day voyage down the coast of France and Spain to a life of slavery in Algiers. This is the story of that horrendous voyage and their new lives as slaves in North Africa before they were ransomed fifteen years later by the English Parliament.

"Raw, emotional and gripping are the best words for me to describe it. It was one of those "just one more chapter" scenarios at two o'clock in the morning." BookSirens

"A wonderful read!" Shonna Froebel, Canadian Bookworm

"A skillfully rendered fictional account of an obscure but fascinating slice of history." Kirkus Reviews

www.ingramcontent.com/pod-product-compliance
Lightning Source LLC
Chambersburg PA
CBHW021052080526
44587CB00010B/228